1005158652

A Handbook of Ethical Practice

CHANDOS
INFORMATION PROFESSIONAL SERIES

Series Editor: Ruth Rikowski
(email: Rikowskigr@aol.com)

Chandos' new series of books are aimed at the busy information professional. They have been specially commissioned to provide the reader with an authoritative view of current thinking. They are designed to provide easy-to-read and (most importantly) practical coverage of topics that are of interest to librarians and other information professionals. If you would like a full listing of current and forthcoming titles, please visit our web site **www.chandospublishing.com** or contact Hannah Grace-Williams on email info@chandospublishing.com or telephone number +44 (0) 1865 884447.

New authors: we are always pleased to receive ideas for new titles; if you would like to write a book for Chandos, please contact Dr Glyn Jones on email gjones@chandospublishing.com or telephone number +44 (0) 1865 884447.

Bulk orders: some organisations buy a number of copies of our books. If you are interested in doing this, we would be pleased to discuss a discount. Please contact Hannah Grace-Williams on email info@chandospublishing.com or telephone number +44 (0) 1865 884447.

A Handbook of
Ethical Practice

*A practical guide to dealing with ethical
issues in information and library work*

DAVID MCMENEMY, ALAN POULTER
AND PAUL F. BURTON

Chandos Publishing
Oxford · England

Chandos Publishing (Oxford) Limited
Chandos House
5 & 6 Steadys Lane
Stanton Harcourt
Oxford OX29 5RL
UK
Tel: +44 (0) 1865 884447 Fax: +44 (0) 1865 884448
Email: info@chandospublishing.com
www.chandospublishing.com

First published in Great Britain in 2007

ISBN:
978 1 84334 230 4 (paperback)
978 1 84334 231 1 (hardback)
1 84334 230 8 (paperback)
1 84334 231 6 (hardback)

© David McMenemy, Alan Poulter and Paul F. Burton, 2007

British Library Cataloguing-in-Publication Data.
A catalogue record for this book is available from the British Library.

Typeset by Avocet Typeset, Chilton, Aylesbury, Bucks.
Printed in the UK and USA.

This book is respectfully dedicated to the *John Doe* librarians:

George Christian, Barbara Bailey, Peter Chase and Janet Nocek
of Library Connection, Windsor, Connecticut, USA

It is one thing to write or preach about ethics, it is quite another
to practise them.

Contents

List of abbreviations   *xi*

Preface   *xiii*

About the authors   *xvii*

1   A taxonomy of the ethics of information use   1

     Ethics and information   1

     Ethics and information use   3

     A taxonomy of general ethical issues relating to information   5

2   The librarian and ethics   7

     The nature of information   7

     Why should librarians be concerned with ethics?   8

     Ethical decision-making   9

     Ethical influences on librarians   11

     Doing the right thing?   14

     The librarian's responsibilities to customers and society   15

     Access and privacy issues   17

     Intellectual property issues   21

     Ethical management of the organisation and the individual   22

     Conclusion   24

3   Ethical codes – an international overview   27

     The need for ethical codes in professions   28

     What the codes specify – an international overview   28

     Conclusion   41

4   **The ethics of information supply – from selection to provision**   **43**

    Selection   43

    Purchasing   45

    Cataloguing and classification   46

    Delivery of information   48

    Case studies   52

    Case study discussions   58

5   **Intellectual property questions**   **65**

    What is intellectual property?   66

    IPR and libraries   67

    Traditional roles versus modern challenges   68

    Balancing rights with responsibilities – electronic dimensions   70

    Conclusion   73

    Case studies   74

    Case study discussions   79

6   **Freedom of access, privacy and acceptable use**   **85**

    Equity of access   86

    Barriers to access   88

    Privacy   89

    User privacy when using library materials   90

    Privacy of the user's personal data   92

    Privacy and the war on terror   94

    Conclusion   95

    Case studies   96

    Case study discussions   101

7   **Ethical management of the self, the individual and the organisation**   **107**

    Management of the self – continuing professional development   108

    Utilising professional networks – discussion lists   110

    Management issues – taking responsibility   111

Managing change effectively – ethical impossibility?   111

Management of the individual   113

Conclusion   114

Case studies   114

Case study discussions   120

8   Conclusion – ethical futures   **125**

Information provision   126

Intellectual property   127

Privacy and equity of access   128

Ethical management   128

The future   129

References   **131**

Suggested readings on ethics in librarianship   **137**

Index   *149*

List of abbreviations

ALA	American Library Association
ALIA	Australian Library and Information Association
AUP	acceptable use policy
CILIP	Chartered Institute of Library and Information Professionals
CPD	continuing professional development
CLA	Canadian Library Association
CLA	Copyright Licensing Agency (UK)
DCMS	Department of Culture, Media and Sport
DRM	digital rights management
IFLA	International Federation of Library Associations
IPR	intellectual property rights
ICT	information and communication technology
LA	Library Association (UK)
LIS	library and information services/science
LIANZA	Library and Information Association of New Zealand Aotearoa
LMS	library management system
NSL	National Security Letter (US)
RIPA	Regulation of Investigatory Powers Act 2000
SLIS	School of Library and Information Science, University of North Texas

Preface

This book was conceived through a desire on the part of the authors to create a practical work that brought together all of the ethical issues that impact on librarianship in the twenty-first century into one discursive text. Teaching ethical issues is notoriously difficult, given that the human race is made up of individuals who possess unique values and beliefs and that decisions made by one may not necessarily be made by another. Deciding what is the right or wrong thing to do is not always a straightforward choice in a private context, therefore knowing what to do in a public context when your decisions are being made on behalf of a user community is challenging. The hope for this book is that it raises these issues in a useful way and that the many challenges faced by librarians when delivering a service can at least be aired for better understanding.

Ethics are an important thing to have: to be accused of being unethical is a term of insult, and to be accused of being an unethical professional is doubly so. Library and information services (LIS) professionals and paraprofessionals face a number of day-to-day challenges that impact on their ability to perform their duties. Providing a service that is based around provision of access to information will understandably present situations where the nature of the information being sought raises some eyebrows. A prolific writer on ethics in librarianship, Robert Hauptman, conducted such an experiment in 1975 when he visited 13 libraries and requested from the reference librarian information on how to create a bomb capable of destroying a suburban home (Hauptman, 1976). To their credit, or discredit depending on your ethical viewpoint, all 13 libraries responded with the information requested. Certainly, 30 years on from this small experiment it is difficult to see how it could be repeated in the current political climate. Cognisant of the world situation and the laws now in place to combat global terrorism, a curious discoverer of the truth would be unwise to undertake a similar request of librarians lest the authorities be called down on him or her. As times change, so perhaps do the ethical concerns of librarians – or do they?

Yet while the 13 librarians in Hauptman's case study could be charged with being naive, they provided information that was in the public domain on request. As librarians they passed a test, but did they do so as citizens? If the answer is no, then what grounds would they have to refuse such a request? Moral indignation in and of itself is not an adequate reason to refuse such a request, and unless they had implicit knowledge that a crime was being committed (it is not necessarily a crime to blow up your own house!) then on what basis could they refuse the request? Several questions and a struggle to find answers to them reflect many of the ethical issues related to information and library work.

Hauptman's experiment resonates in the twenty-first century just as it did in the late twentieth. While not all ethical dilemmas will mirror those tested by Hauptman, there are numerous scenarios dealt with day in and day out by LIS professionals that offer ethical dilemmas. There is often no practical ethical guidance available, save senior colleagues or other professional networks of support, and even these may pose more questions than answers. Many professional associations representing librarians have attempted to codify these challenges within their documented ethical principles (as will be discussed in Chapter 3), although many of these codes are general in scope, and there remains a need for a fuller discussion of the ethical issues that face LIS professionals based around real-world ethical dilemmas.

Therefore the aim of this book is to discuss the ethical issues facing LIS workers in the modern era. The discussion will be based around:

- a review of the key ethical challenges faced by LIS professionals both contemporaneously and historically;
- an examination of some of the ethical codes adopted by professional LIS associations;
- discussion of case studies based around the key ethical themes identified.

A significant emphasis of the book will be on casuistry, one definition of which is the discussion of ethics via scenarios or case studies. Large portions of many of the chapters are given over to case studies, but rather than painting a scenario and asking questions, the case studies ask the reader to make ethical choices for each scenario. Each of these ethical choices will lead to a discussion of the ethical implications of the choice taken. All case studies will be preceded by a discussion of the ethical theories involved, but the authors feel that the real value for the reader will be in thinking about the case studies and the responses they believe are apt. That most of the case studies have multiple potential responses is interesting, and it is certainly not our intention to state categorically which choices are right and which wrong, although we will hopefully discuss the potential implications of each choice in enough detail that the reader can decide which choices are wiser than others.

It is important to note that this book is not attempting to offer legal advice; instead it will attempt to present the ethical themes of concern to LIS professionals and the complex natures of their challenges, with a detailed discussion of a mixture of real-life and imaginary case studies based around the potential solutions adopted in the front-line of LIS work. It is hoped that students of LIS find the book useful in their studies of the ethical issues facing them in their new profession, and that tutors teaching ethics or professional issues to library students or staff find the case studies of use in highlighting the issues. It is also hoped that the scenarios presented will proffer guidance to LIS professionals who may be facing an ethical challenge for the first time and who would like to understand the potential solutions that could be adopted and the decision-making process that arrived at those solutions. Equally it is hoped that LIS professionals who may previously have come across the ethical challenges discussed will be able to use the case studies in their own decision-making and professional development.

The authors have a combined experience of over 50 years in information and library work both in professional roles and as academics teaching librarianship, and hope that the discussions that follow are both helpful and informative, and offer at the very least an opportunity for the reader to engage further with the ethical dilemmas they may face in their day-to-day work.

David McMenemy, Alan Poulter and Paul F. Burton
Glasgow, Scotland, July 2006

About the authors

David McMenemy BA (Hons), MSc, MCLIP, ILTM has been a Lecturer in the Department of Computer and Information Sciences at the University of Strathclyde since 2001. His previous experience includes ten years working in public libraries in Glasgow, Scotland, where he had a range of roles from reference work, to community libraries, to working on the roll out of the People's Network in the city's libraries.

David is the winner of the 2006 Elsevier/CILIP Research Award for his investigation into the barriers in place to Internet use in UK public libraries. He is Editor of *Library Review*, and is involved with several aspects of the business of CILIP, including being an External Examiner for the Chartership Board and being a member of the Scottish branch's Council.

David is co-author with Alan Poulter of *Delivering Digital Services: A Handbook for Public Libraries and Learning Centres* and *The Library and Information Professional's Internet Companion*.

Alan Poulter BA, MA, MSc, MCLIP has been a Lecturer in the Department of Computer and Information Sciences at the University of Strathclyde since 2001.

His previous career includes working as a cataloguer and indexer at the British Library and database/thesaurus manager at the Science Museum. He has been a university lecturer in library and information science for over 15 years. He has published books and numerous academic papers, and given conference papers on library and IT-related topics: public libraries, cataloguing/metadata, digital libraries, Internet technologies, information systems and databases. He is Editor of *ITALICS: Innovations in Teaching and Learning in Information and Computer Sciences*, an Associate Editor of *Library Review* and an editorial board member for the *Journal of Internet Cataloging*.

In a professional capacity he is Secretary of the Library and Information Research Group of CILIP and a member of the Assessment Panel for CILIP Scotland.

Paul F. Burton BA, MA, MPhil, PhD, FCLIP has been a Senior Lecturer at the University of Strathclyde since 1985.

His research and teaching interests encompass a wide range of issues relating to technology and libraries and ethical issues. He also teaches courses and has interests in reference services, digital libraries, and legal and policy issues of information and library work.

Previous professional library experience includes higher education, public libraries and college libraries. In addition Paul has published several books in the past, including *Information Management Technology: A Librarian's Guide* and *Micro-computers for Information Management* (both with J. Howard Petrie) and *Information Technology and Society: Implications for the Information Professions.*

The authors may be contacted via the publishers.

A taxonomy of the ethics of information use

Ethics and information

This chapter performs an essential grounding function. It introduces the two concepts of ethics and information and endeavours to try to generalise the types of ethical problem encountered when information is produced, used or destroyed. The intent is to produce a basic taxonomy of ethical problem types in information use. This taxonomy will help clarify thinking and discourse about ethical issues in information use, underpin the structure of the discussion of ethical issues in the following chapters and form a means to organise materials on ethical issues in information use, as, for example, in the case studies this book will later use to give readers and students the task of dealing with ethical issues.

Firstly, let us consider what we mean by the term ethics. Ethics is a branch of philosophical enquiry; primarily it relates to the choices made and actions undertaken by the individual and how they impact on wider society. The word itself and the philosophical concept can be traced back to the teachings of Socrates. Etymologically the word is derived from the Greek *ethikos*, which refers to moral duty. It is important at this juncture to note that ethical issues and legal issues, while occasionally intersecting each other, are distinct concepts. For instance, it may be immoral and therefore unethical to uphold a specific law. Conversely, something that is deemed illegal may actually be ethical and moral. Another way of viewing the dichotomy between ethics and law is to consider that, at root, ethics are enforced by the conscience of the individual while laws are ultimately enforced by the physical power of governmental organisations. One would hope that ethics and laws would coincide, since their common wellspring is the conscience of individuals. It is important to note that this book does not aim to give legal advice but does aim to investigate the ethics of information use.

If ethics is a concept that is widely understood, the same cannot be said for the term 'information'. The meaning of the word 'information' is not clear, as in everyday usage the word is employed extremely loosely. In general terms information can have four aspects:

- as a feature of the environment, e.g. a thunder cloud;
- as a by-product of human communication, e.g. gossip;
- as an economic commodity, the production costs of which need to be covered by sales, e.g. a newspaper, a television broadcast;
- as a discrete resource, e.g. a manuscript.

While the last aspect above is the one that most commonly springs to mind as information, the others are also important. These aspects are not completely distinct: for example, a book combines the aspects of discrete resource and economic commodity. A road sign is both an environmental feature and a discrete resource. A letter is both a discrete resource and a communication by-product, and so on.

Digitisation serves to blur boundaries even further. A blog combines communication by-product and discrete resource and may even encompass economic commodity if it charges readers. The Internet provides access to environmental features (e.g. via webcams and satellite images), oceans of gossip in chat, e-mail and online conferences and billions of discrete web pages. Not only does digitisation blur boundaries between aspects of information, it also transforms hitherto different physical forms into one universal representation: bytes. This universal form is simple to create using software tools, easy to copy or duplicate and can be very quickly moved around using digital networks.

Digitisation has affected the economic commodity aspect of information most. An individual with a camcorder can create a digital copy of a first-run film he or she has watched in a cinema, upload that single copy to the Internet and, through copy after copy being downloaded, severely dent future cinema and DVD revenues for that film. Conversely, a film in digital format can be sold in a protected form which prevents it being copied or used on anything other than one particular device and the act of purchase can be turned into one of rental, as the digital film can periodically require a top-up subscription payment to play. Creators of information can both have no control and total control over their creations.

Individuals have always generated information about themselves, and had others generate information about them. Again, digitisation has enabled greater extremes than before. On one hand, individuals can be tagged and tracked by satellite and phone calls and Internet use can be tracked, recorded and automatically analysed, while personal information can be hijacked and used to embarrass an individual or enable someone else to effectively impersonate them. On the other hand, encryption makes it possible for information about crimes or obscene behaviour to be scrambled beyond any hope of recovery and technically adept individuals can exploit the vulnerability of digital data about them for their own ends.

Ethics and information use

We all need information to go about our daily lives. Even primitive hunter-gatherers needed to know a lot about the features of their environment. Ancient monuments like Stonehenge show how valuable a simple calendar was to the people that carefully arranged its giant stones. Nowadays, individuals still need information about their locality, such as the location of the nearest ATM, except that now this information can come via specialised mobile phone services as well as from wandering the streets and searching. Everyone needs access to information.

However there are some factors which can affect the need to access information. Firstly, although digitisation can potentially remove cost, there is still going to be some form of resourcing issue. For example, the Internet is an enormous repository of (mostly) freely available information. However, to access that information one needs some form of digital device, a usable connection to the Internet and the requisite knowledge and skills. Second, despite digitisation, some information sources will be unique: for example, historical documents like the Magna Carta can be digitised but there is still something extra to be gleaned from contact with the original.

There are also factors which can create blocks on information access. Some information may be inappropriate for certain people. For example, should a five-year-old child be looking at pornography? Some information is very dangerous. Bombs can be constructed from commonplace materials. Weapons of mass destruction can be made using contagious, lethal bacteria or highly poisonous chemicals. Determining what information can be dangerous in particular circumstances is very arduous. Information is also difficult to control, so any would-be blocks are necessarily somewhat porous.

Information does not come naturally accessible. Books do not arrange themselves on shelves, web pages need to be discovered. Information is hard to organise. Any particular piece of information can be useful in a variety of ways to different people at different times. Trying to consistently recognise the usefulness of information resources in a variety of contexts and for different uses is not a skill that comes naturally. Information resources come with basic finding aids – a title to identify it, a statement of responsibility for its creation, etc. Beyond the creator of an information resource, others may play a part in describing that information resource – the publisher, the retailer, the custodian and sometimes even the information user. Digitisation affects this chain by blurring boundaries between links, so that, for example, creator, publisher and retailer may be one entity.

Digitisation has also vastly increased the amount of information created. Lyman and Varian (2003) state that in 2002:

- 5 exabytes of new, unique data was produced, 800 Mb per person;
- 92 per cent of this was stored on magnetic disks;
- the Web contained 172 terabytes, 17 times the size of the Library of Congress's print collections;
- e-mail generated 400,000 terabytes of data.

If their estimate that the amount of new information appeared was to double annually, how can any individual hope to deal with this deluge? Is there not a pressing need here for a class of information specialist to take on the business of finding relevant information to meet expressed needs from less skilled individuals? The role of mediator brings with it inherent problems. Can a mediator really understand the needs and wishes of others? Is there not a danger that a mediator might (consciously or unconsciously) interfere with or even prevent an individual getting needed information? Can a mediator ever justify recommending, with the best of intentions, information that an individual has not requested and may not want? Can a mediator ever justify withholding information that an individual has requested and wants? Returning to the original problem of information overload, mediators will be affected by this as well: can a mediator effectively deal with information outside their domain of competency?

A taxonomy of general ethical issues relating to information

By reducing the previous discussion to its bare essentials we can propose the following general statements about ethical issues that relate to information:

1. How can the concept of information be defined so as to clearly reveal its ethical implications?

2. How much control should the creator of information have over that information?

3. How much control should an individual have about the information that pertains to him or her?

4. Do individuals have the right to access any piece of information they need?

5. Is there a duty to make certain information inaccessible when appropriate?

6. Is there a duty to make information fully accessible and findable?

7. Is there a need for a mediator between an individual and the information they seek?

The librarian and ethics

The nature of information

As discussed in the previous chapter, information has been defined as a commodity, meaning that it is something that can be both bought and sold, and is something that has value to the owner or receiver (Feather, 2004). This value need not be expressed in monetary terms. For instance, a common enquiry in reference libraries is the search for the full text of a poem or a song from the requester's knowledge of a single line. Identifying the work for a patron will not normally have any monetary value for them or the library, but it may well bring great happiness and satisfaction to the person, especially if the poem or song has some sentimental value. This kind of value is very difficult to measure. A satisfaction survey may tick all of the correct boxes, but it cannot express the positive benefit that small piece of information may have had for the person.

Yet, expanding on the discussion from the previous chapter, what exactly is information and how does its various forms influence the ethical issues facing librarians? Librarians across sectors provide information to hugely diverse client groups, for a myriad of purposes and in a plethora of different formats. Traditional public librarianship involves everything from lending books to providing community information, newspapers, bus timetables and recommendations on lending choices. The academic librarian may also provide a lot of the same services, but also be deeply concerned with supporting the learning of the students. Corporate librarians are interested in supplying information that will enhance the performance of the company. While the backbone in all three sectors is ensuring clients receive the information they need, the ethical challenges involved in each can differ enormously.

Why should librarians be concerned with ethics?

Let us begin by examining why ethics should be important to librarians. Ethical standards are central to the sphere of activity of any profession. Indeed, labelling someone as a professional implies that they understand all there is to know about their chosen trade, not merely the skills for the job, but the ability to practise those skills to an agreed standard. As Hannabuss has observed:

> Professional standards lead people to believe that their enquiries will be dealt with competently and confidentially, that prejudice or bias will not be shown, that appropriate care will be taken over sensitive material (particularly for clients who appear to be susceptible to their effects), and that people of all social types and groups will be dealt with without favouritism. (Hannabuss, 1998: 93)

Such standards are crucial not merely for professional competency; the dangers of not knowing the ethical way of doing things may impact on the employer and even wider society. As Sturges has stated, 'it has become vital that ethical awareness is cultivated from the moment of entry into a profession and throughout the career' (Sturges, 2003: 101). The potential ramifications of a professional performing any task without due care for ethical standards may be to the detriment of individual people or groups, and could have profound legal consequences for the professional concerned and the employing organisation. This is as true in library and information work as in any other, especially in the digital age, when issues of organisation, storage and dissemination take on an added dimension.

Despite being a profession that is centuries old, the literature on ethical issues in librarianship is sparse before the 1970s (Hauptman, 1988). Certainly questions remain as to why the library profession did not consider the issue of ethics important enough to consider codifying before the efforts of the American Library Association (ALA) in 1938. In the UK, the Library Association (LA) did not adopt an ethical code until 1983, over 100 years after it was formed as a professional association. There is a school of thought that suggests the complacency of the profession in this regard was based as much on society's ignorance of what librarians actually do as much as our lack of desire to define an ethical benchmark for professionals in our industry. Writing in the mid-1980s Lindsey and Prentice suggest that:

> The average person is highly unlikely to have given a second – or even a first – thought to the question of the professional ethics of librarians. Think of the stereotype of a librarian: a bespectacled spinster with a pencil in her bun, dispensing novels to drowsy dowagers and shushing rowdy students. What could *that* image have to do with ethics at all? (Lindsey and Prentice, 1985: vii)

Stereotype or not, ethical questions have faced librarians since the profession began. In the example above, even the act of 'shushing' is in and of itself an ethical choice, as the dispensing of novels to the dowager could be if said novel is controversial or promotes themes that are deemed unsavoury or illegal in the jurisdiction within which the library operates. Ethical decisions may have been something that was merely seen as a day-to-day necessity by many LIS professionals, but they have been central concerns since the dawn of the profession, codified or not.

Ethical decision-making

It is important at this juncture to reinforce the point that ethical issues and legal issues, while occasionally intersecting each other, are distinct concepts. Ironically, in extreme circumstances it may be seen as unethical to uphold a specific law when providing a service. These types of situations, although relatively uncommon historically, are increasing as legislation is passed that attempts to limit freedoms historically provided. For example, controversy surrounds such recent acts as the Patriot Act 2001 in the USA and the Regulation of Investigatory Powers Act 2000 (RIPA) in the UK, both of which potentially impact on the privacy of library patrons. A recent high-profile case in the USA saw four senior library professionals in Connecticut raise a case against the government over the legality of the Patriot Act. Specifically they were challenging the legality of what is known as a National Security Letter or NSL, which compels the receiver to hand over information to law enforcement, after which they are not allowed to tell anyone about the request In the case of the 'John Doe' librarians (as they became known, as their identities could not be revealed) they were asked to provide statistics on Internet use from one of the library terminals. The case brought much publicity, and has only recently been resolved by the government dropping the case (Library Journal, 2006). The decision taken by the John Doe librarians was a brave one, and certainly an ethical one. They were defending historic rights to privacy that librarians have protected for generations. Yet in a climate that allows legislation such as the Patriot Act to be passed, a stance like that of the John Doe librarians may be challenging to sustain. Doing the ethical thing may well lead to criticism and condemnation from others who do not share the same beliefs.

Many observers, including many librarians, remain unconvinced with regard to the morality of legislation such as the Patriot Act, therefore adhering to these laws when providing a service may well be legal, but to them would be unethical from a personal or professional point of view, or both. As Hauptman has stated, librarians should 'fight against abrogations and restrictions on access' to information (Hauptman, 1988: 79). The librarians in Connecticut took their ethical responsibilities seriously enough that they challenged what they believed to be an unethical law. The restrictions on freedom put in place in the western world as a result of the war on terror have great implications for the library profession. While most of the headlines have been devoted to the Patriot Act in the USA, in the UK and Australia a more robust interest on the part of governments for what citizens are doing, and limiting it, is evident (Andrews, 2002). The Chartered Institute of Library and Information Professionals (CILIP) has been advised that various Acts, including RIPA and the Terrorism Act 2000, could be used to obtain records of borrowing and to carry out surveillance in libraries of all types. Speaking at CILIP's annual conference in October 2005, CILIP's President Deborah Shorley noted that the profession had a responsibility to help to protect society against terrorism, but also added that 'We have a duty of client confidentiality and so we cannot collude with fishing expeditions by the authorities' (CILIP, 2006a). Proposed new legislation in the form of the Terrorism Act 2006 could, it was suggested, have been used to prosecute library and information workers whose libraries held material which the authorities regarded as assisting in acts of terrorism. The Act has subsequently been amended to include the concepts of 'intent' or 'recklessness', which should protect library staff (CILIP, 2006b).

Libraries offer access to reading materials, and in many cases free Internet access. They normally do so on the basis of an expectation of reasonable privacy, or at least we have historically afforded that courtesy. As Gorman has stated:

On moral grounds, we must begin with the premise that everyone is entitled to freedom of access, freedom to read texts and view images, and freedom of thought and expression. None of those freedoms can survive in an atmosphere in which library use is monitored and individual reading and library use patterns are made known to anyone without permission. (Gorman, 2000: 151)

Gorman was writing a year before the horrors of September 11th, and his words certainly echo the experiences of the John Doe librarians. Equally there will be many people who argue that since 9/11 the world has changed and the ethics of librarians must change with it.

Ethical influences on librarians

This brings us to a crucial point in relation to the discussion of professional ethics. Notwithstanding the legal aspects of providing an ethical service, there are four other issues that can potentially impact on the ethical decision-making of the library and information science (LIS) professional and the subsequent ability to provide a service to the customer. These are (see Figure 2.1):

Figure 2.1   Ethical influences on librarians

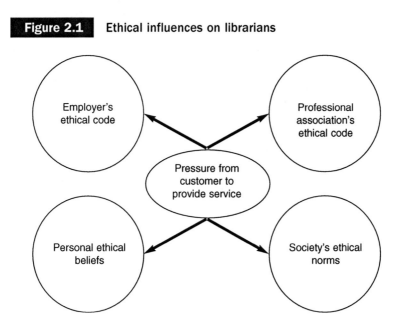

- the ethical code/ethos of the employer;
- the ethical code of the professional association of which the professional is a member;
- the personal ethical viewpoint of the individual professional;
- wider views of society relating to the ethical questions faced by the professional.

The employer

It may well be the case that an individual does not share the same ethical viewpoint as that of his or her employer on many issues. This is not necessarily an issue that will lead to controversy unless such difference of opinion manifests itself in the refusal on behalf of the employee to deliver a service. It may be the case, for instance, that a librarian works for a public library service that is governed by a political party they did not vote for. This may in turn present issues if the politics of the governing body begin to influence library provision and the librarian is then tasked with implementing policy he or she disagrees with. This is equally so if the librarian works for a corporate body that may undertake work of a potentially controversial nature, such as the oil industry or pharmaceuticals. There is little to be said for getting a job in an organisation where the individual knows his or her ethics will be constantly tested by the nature of the work the organisation undertakes, but certainly, having done so, the professional will find pressure to deliver a quality service. From a political point of view, in the United Kingdom it was illegal for 15 years between 1988 and 2003 for homosexuality to be 'promoted' by local government services. As a national government diktat this meant that regardless of the political persuasion of your local government (the branch of government responsible for public libraries) it was illegal to promote the homosexual lifestyle. The amendment to the 1988 Local Government Act that brought in the clause, commonly referred to as Clause 28, stated that local authorities 'shall not intentionally promote homosexuality or publish material with the intention of promoting homosexuality.' This led to fears that public libraries stocking titles with positive homosexual characters or themes may be potentially liable for prosecution. When such a mindset of fear is allowed to develop it hinders service and runs the risk that an entire social grouping of library users sees their lives blocked from library bookshelves.

The professional association

Ethical codes and how they impact on the work of LIS professionals will be discussed in detail in the next chapter. At this point it is important to note that ethical dilemmas faced on the front line may not necessarily be informed by reference to ethical codes, since they work as mission statements rather than practical tools. For the most part they embody a set of *principles* which librarians adhere to, but they offer little in the way of guidance from the point of view of *practical tasks*. This is not necessarily something they can be criticised for; it is important for a profession to communicate its vision for ethical practice not merely to members but also in laypersons' terms in order that the public can understand what drives and underpins the professional ethos. However, it continues to be a challenge exactly how ethical codes can be made directly relevant to the working lives of an association's members. Indeed, the key question is whether they need to be relevant in this way or whether setting an ethical benchmark is all they are required to do.

Personal beliefs/ethical views

Librarianship is a profession made up of individuals from many ethnic groups and creeds. It is inevitable that ethical viewpoints will be different across cultures and that on occasion providing access to a piece of information may well pose personal issues for the individual librarian. How severe this dilemma is can vary, but in theory it could present a scenario that is a simple choice between the ethical view of the librarian and the act of providing a service. Such a case was witnessed in the UK in late 2005 when a library worker in a Welsh town refused to serve a customer who had previously been banned for surfing in a sex chatroom (BBC News, 2005). The man concerned had served the library-imposed ban for breaching the Internet acceptable use policy, and thus by the library regulations should have been allowed access to library services again. By not serving the customer the library worker concerned was in breach of library regulations and was essentially placing her own ethical values before those of the library authority. Rightly or wrongly, her stance was not welcomed by either the customer or the library authority, and a written apology was sent to the customer.

Society's beliefs/ethical views

It is often the case that society is ahead of legislation on many social issues. This may lead to restrictions on services within a library appearing old-fashioned or ill-judged, and such restrictions may put the LIS professional in the front line of complaints about it. Equally the service being provided may be deemed to be avant-garde by wider society and restrictions may be placed on it by a concerned populace or officials acting in their interests.

Such an issue occurred in 1997 in the UK city of Birmingham when a student undertaking a project investigating the concept of fine art versus pornography took some photographs taken from a university textbook to their local chemist to be developed. The photographs contained images from a book chronicling the work of controversial photographer Robert Mapplethorpe, and were reported to the local police by a staff member in the chemist. Police seized the book from the library citing legislation that suggested the photographs were obscene. Despite an ongoing controversy that lasted over a year, the university hierarchy stood by the principle of free speech and in the end the decision was taken not to prosecute (University of Central England, 1999). Fortunately in this case the university took the appropriate stance for a learned institution and defended the right of free speech. The ethical dilemma was faced by an entire institution, with management support, but supposing the incident occurred in an organisation where such support was not forthcoming or was piecemeal? In Chapter 4 the issue of banning books and the ethical dilemmas this places on librarians will be discussed in more detail.

Doing the right thing?

To paraphrase an article title by Sturges a little, the relation of ethical enquiry to professionalism generally is that of doing the right thing (Sturges, 2003). Yet defining the 'right thing' is not always easy. In the Hauptman bomb experiment cited earlier, the right thing for the user was to provide the information requested; if that request had subsequently led to the creation of a bomb and lives were lost or another crime committed, then a publicly funded institution could have been culpable. Doing the right thing is not always perceived to be the correct action by those outside of the profession. In the twenty-first century and for the same enquiry as Hauptman undertook in the 1970s, doing the right thing may be to ensure that anyone requesting information on bomb-making is reported to the police. Yet this would understandably leave a bad taste in the mouth for many in the library profession. It is unlikely, however, to do so for the majority of the general public – and therein lies the fundamental dilemma.

On another note, professional ethics are about ensuring a reflective approach to one's own practice. The issue of reflective practice has grown in popularity in recent years, focusing on the ability of individuals to look at their behaviour and performance critically, and improve it where necessary. Yet ethical decision-making often has to occur at the point of service delivery and, in the case of developing rules and regulations for service quality and access to services, before the delivery of a service has occurred. There is often very little time at the front line, if any, to reflect on the scenario faced. Decisions may have to be split second, and may be influenced by a myriad of issues, as evidenced above.

The librarian's responsibilities to customers and society

As an ethical starting point LIS professionals should recognise their fundamental importance in helping to develop the information society; this is absolutely crucial. Indeed this is exactly what librarians have been attempting to do, long before the concept of an information society had been developed. In medicine doctors have the Hippocratic Oath: for the librarian the closest creed we have are the principles espoused in 1931 by S.R. Ranganathan, namely:

1. Books are for use.
2. For every reader, his or her book.
3. For every book, its reader.
4. Save the time of the reader.
5. A library is a growing organism. (Ranganathan, 1931)

While the terminology is historically grounded – we would need to include more than books in the twenty-first century version of the five laws – the ethical backbone such principles provide are as relevant today as they were in 1931. Ranganathan has been interpreted exhaustively over the years since his five laws were first published, but a simple translation of them for the modern era would be that we must encourage all potential users to access information; that regardless of creed or colour there is something a library has that will be of value to a customer; that we ensure that the way we organise and store the material is for the benefit of the user and not our own; and that we continue to add to the collections we make available to people. At the heart of Ranganathan's laws are the universal notions of equity of access to, and availability of, information for all.

Recently Michael Gorman has made an attempt to revisit the guiding principles and values of librarianship: he has identified eight themes that he calls our enduring values:

1. Stewardship
2. Service
3. Intellectual freedom
4. Equity of access
5. Privacy
6. Literacy and learning
7. Rationalism
8. Democracy. (Gorman, 2000)

Gorman's ethos mirrors that of Ranganathan, yet he articulates a fuller set of principles for the modern era. The themes of intellectual freedom and rationalism play to a world where both are continuously under threat. Democracy as an enduring value of librarianship is a controversial point, since there are many librarians across the globe who do not live or work in democracies; indeed they could be argued as espousing western values in that regard. Gorman's values are interesting because they combine a twin track of service delivery and professional influence – not merely the act of issuing a book or a piece of information, but knowing that, by doing so, you are contributing to a larger goal, be it the literacy of the individual, the intellectual freedom of the author, or the rationalism of society fighting against religious censorship. The values laid down by both Ranganathan and Gorman are attempts to give librarians a set of guiding principles, and we will constantly revisit these themes within the wider discussion and the case studies to follow.

Therefore LIS professionals should consider their position in terms of benefit to their wider client base, be this public or commercial; however, all should feel some responsibility for promoting the notion of free and equal access to information for all. It is quite simply the fundamental reason for the existence of the profession, and is increasingly necessary in the current world climate.

Yet standing as information intermediary brings some major ethical challenges, especially in the digital age. These challenges can be broadly categorised into three macro themes:

1. Access and privacy

2. Intellectual property

3. Ethical management of the individual and the organisation.

These themes and their micro themes will be discussed in more detail below with a view to placing the case study chapters in context.

Access and privacy issues

Librarians have historically made information available to customers. Access to information is not a straightforward process. Material must be selected, processed for use and then made available. Availability in itself is not straightforward; is the piece of information restricted by the physicality of the library building? In addition, while a book may be available in one library, access rights to that library may be highly limited to a small membership group based on location or another rubric.

Gateways or barriers

As discussed, provision of access to information should be a core aim for most LIS professionals regardless of the sector they find themselves in. Be the user a member of the public visiting a community library, a student visiting a college library or a nurse visiting a hospital library, the fundamental goal is the same: provision of the information source the user is seeking. On top of this may also be the necessity to aid clients in their use of the resource or in understanding the resource. In this context LIS professionals are often likened to gatekeepers. Yet the term gatekeeper also has negative connotations. Gates are designed both as entry points and as barriers, and one of the ethical challenges facing LIS professionals is the extent to which they limit or prevent access not only to those outwith their client group, but to those within. As will be discussed below, intellectual property rights tend to be one of the major concerns in this context, but others are also prominent. For example, in the modern context let us consider the issue of Internet filtering.

The Internet is the primary information tool of the twenty-first century and its importance will only grow as it becomes increasingly sophisticated and as users become more reliant on it for their day-to-day needs. The Internet user accessing from home comes to expect relatively unlimited access to the information contained on the billions of pages available, but this is problematic for libraries for several reasons.

Internet filtering is the software-driven process of excluding websites from being able to be accessed on a computer and is used by many libraries to prevent users from accessing specific categories of website. The process is normally driven by the blocking of words or phrases within the text of a web page, or via a web address which is on a list of banned sites, or a combination of both. The rationale for filtering is perfectly sound from a specific ethical standpoint; it is about the prevention of access to inappropriate materials, especially inappropriate materials that may well be illegal, such as specific types of pornography. Yet the basis of Internet filtering is the antithesis of free and open access. This is a major ethical question for a LIS professional, since, in addition to the issue of free and open access, and despite the knowledge that some material accessed on the Internet may be unsuitable for users, there is the equal concern that legitimate material may be blocked by filtering software. This becomes even more of a concern when we consider the nature of the legitimate material blocked, such as material on sexual health, breast cancer or sexuality. One argument posited is that all a user need do is ask the librarian to unblock any legitimate material that is being withheld by the filtering software, but this is a naive argument. Consider how many users may be too embarrassed to ask a librarian about issues like sexuality – indeed this may be the primary reason why they have chosen the Internet as their information source as it offers relative anonymity and privacy. Being confronted with a screen blocking access to information is unlikely to have such a user politely chatting to the librarian to have their information provided, regardless of the librarian's approachability.

Freedom of access

The right of access to information has been defined as a fundamental human right (IFLA, 2000). It can often be easy in the western world, where public libraries have existed for over 100 years, to forget how fortunate we are to have community resources where the public can access information at no cost. The more information a public library is able to provide to its community, the more democratic that community will be. It is common, for instance, to have public libraries making available government papers and minutes to the public, allowing the community to engage with their leaders. Freedom of access to information is crucial for a democracy to thrive, and libraries are often the only easily accessible source of such information for many communities.

Censorship

Censorship is as old as time. Vested interests or prejudices will always see someone seek to limit the spread of a piece of information or a book or other work of intellectual capital. Equally, librarians have continuously sought to ensure that books are made available to the public, but they often face a fight in doing so. Controversy often surrounds artistic works that seek to push the envelope, and the example cited in the Mapplethorpe case discussed above illustrates how seriously the authorities can take such issues. Yet intellectual freedom is fundamental to a democratic system, and librarians should be at the forefront of defending it.

Dangers to intellectual freedom do not always come from the expected sources, for instance fundamentalists or extreme believers. There are many who argue that they are in favour of intellectual freedom yet by their actions suggest something different. As Gorman has observed:

> The fact is that many quarrels about intellectual freedom are not between those who are for it and those who are against it. They are often between people who believe in different applications of intellectual freedom, while all professing to be for it. (Gorman, 2000: 89)

The recent case in 2006 of the cartoons depicting the Prophet Mohammad saw many liberal commentators taking the stance that the publication of the cartoons by European newspapers was indefensible (Sign and Sight, 2006). Yet in doing so, the stance taken is that the right to be offended outweighs the right to offend. This is certainly a route that leads to less controversy but it is not necessarily one that enhances the development of intellectual freedom. Censorship for any reason is a potential slippery slope; if one group in society is able to restrict the expression of creative thought then it follows that others will seek to do so. Hauptman agrees that intellectual freedom should be protected but, 'realistically, stringent limits' should be placed on it. He continues:

> It is easy to insist that one should neither censor nor refuse to disseminate information. It is much more difficult to justify the requested purchase of pornographic videos for a primary school or public library's children's collection, even if one is not personally opposed to these items. (Hauptman, 1988: 71)

Yet within such sensible constraints librarians need to continuously champion the importance of intellectual freedom. As Gorman argues:

> Censorship is anathema to us because it inhibits our role in life – to make the recorded knowledge of humankind freely available to everyone, regardless of faith or the lack of it, ethnicity, gender, age, or any other of the categories that divide us one from another. (Gorman, 2000: 90)

These are challenging times for the pursuit of intellectual freedom, and libraries will face increasing challenges from individuals and groups with vested interests who seek to limit access to materials.

Inappropriate materials

As highlighted above by Hauptman, even the most libertarian mindset would acknowledge that there are many materials that are not suitable for children. In the analogue past where materials were printed, either in book, magazine or photograph format, it was a simple process for a librarian to ensure children did not access material that was inappropriate for them. In the wired world there is no foolproof way of doing so, despite what manufacturers of Internet filtering products may say in order to sell their products. While taking a large portion of the responsibility from the librarian, filtering software is not 100 per cent effective and thus its use needs to be monitored. It is unlikely ever to be the safeguard required for librarians wishing to ensure that children do not access pornography. Therefore, while the librarian has, in this case, the role of educator, ensuring that children know how best to seek out materials appropriate to the them, he or she may also have to adopt the gatekeeper role and ensure that children cannot access inappropriate materials.

Providing wide range of opinion in publications on offer

As the steward of the collected knowledge of mankind, the librarian must ensure that enough of the collected knowledge is available to customers as is practicable. This means that all aspects of intellectual discourse should be available to the enquiring mind, controversial or not. The librarian has a duty to ensure that all viewpoints are accessible for those who wish to seek them out and that, whatever they personally think of an opinion, it is not imparted by them to a customer. It is not the role of a librarian to editorialise on the merits of a piece of information they supply to a customer. Equally the librarian should not lead a customer to a resource for any other reason than customer need. To steer a customer to a particular viewpoint for any other reason than that it is the viewpoint the person is seeking is wholly unethical.

Intellectual property issues

The issues around intellectual property are discussed in detail in Chapter 5. For the moment it is enough to note that the tension that surrounds intellectual property is based on the pressure to protect the creative endeavour that has gone into producing a work versus the librarian's desire to allow access. This tension has existed for as long as there has been commercial publishing, but the digital age makes the challenge a difficult one to manage. The full text of a book can be e-mailed in a second to thousands of recipients across the world, and each recipient can then e-mail it to others. It is not a surprise that publishers of all media, books, CDs, DVDs, have targeted those who breach intellectual property rights with robust legal challenges, but in many ways they can only scratch the surface of the problem by doing so.

The issue that challenges librarians directly is that in their role as gatekeeper they must also ensure that intellectual property rights are not breached under their noses. The ethical aspects of this are twofold: not merely protecting the creative work but also protecting the library from potential legal liability if the publisher discovers any breach for which the library could be held responsible (and we must consider here the circumstances under which the library could be held liable for such breaches). As technology improves and new generations of users with a 'download and share' mindset frequent libraries, this can only become a larger problem for the librarian of the twenty-first century. The librarian runs the risk of becoming merely the intellectual property police officer if he or she does not seek to educate users as to the appropriate respect for and usage of materials.

Ethical management of the organisation and the individual

The discussion so far has focused on those unique ethical issues that relate to the library profession specifically. However, there are issues that all professionals, regardless of the domain, need to address.

Proper management of the organisation and the self is of essential importance for the professional status of an individual. Ethical management of the organisation involves examining issues such as appropriate use of resources and good human resources practice. Ethical management of the self focuses around the issues related to continuing professional development, or CPD as it is more commonly referred to.

Appropriate use of resources

Sturges cites the case of Henry Bond, a librarian from Portsmouth, England, who took his own life in 1917 because of scandals involving embezzlement of funds from the library that were set to end his career (Sturges, 2003: 94). The trust placed on an employee charged with managing public funds is a vital one, and every pound or cent should be cherished and spent for the full benefit of the library user. This is equally true for those librarians who work in the private sector. To be placed in a position of trust where one is charged with purchasing resources for use by others places a heavy responsibility on an individual. To abuse this trust in any way is ethically unacceptable, and may indeed be against the law.

Although not normally legally problematic, to abuse the trust of purchasing materials by buying books or other media only because you favour them personally is also unethical. At least one of the authors of this book knows of a librarian in the past with particular interests who ensured that his library had a significant set of holdings in that topic not through necessity but through personal interest. One school of thought would be that if someone has an interest in a topic and can acquire a thorough collection of materials on that topic that can be shared in a library system, then this is not necessarily an abuse of the system. This is certainly true if that agreement has been made across a library system and authorised by senior management, but if it happens by a librarian abusing the right to purchase by buying material he or she personally favours then the ends do not necessarily justify by the means. By purchasing materials in one topic at the expense of other materials there is a significant chance that library customers are being ill-served.

Librarians and politics

The individual politics of librarians should never influence their service to the public. This is absolutely fundamental and should never be in question. In terms of politics, however, something that librarians do have to guard against is the politicisation of their service. At the moment libraries are at the top of many government agendas across the world because of the growing interest in lifelong learning. This is obviously a wonderful opportunity for libraries to gain fresh resources and deliver better services, but there is also the potential for libraries to go down routes of service where they take their eye off their main roles and risk their future viability. Public librarians especially can often forget just how attractive a proposition they are for others who wish to deliver services using their facilities. The public library network in any region is ready-made, staffed and open at hours that suit many of their customers. This is potentially attractive to other organisations who can complement the services offered by the public library, but there remains a need to ensure that any services invited to use the facilities do indeed complement the existing services. At the very least it should be remembered that governments change, and successive priorities may be different. To place excessive emphasis on a government-sponsored initiative at the expense of traditional services puts a service in potential peril if a new government is elected which ceases the initiative.

Continuing professional development

All professionals should ensure that their professional knowledge is as up to date as it can be. For most professions the entry-level degree, be it Bachelors or Masters, prepares the student to enter the profession of choice. It does not and cannot make the student the complete professional or the finished article, and new entrants to the profession have an ethical duty to ensure they continuously learn about their profession throughout their career.

This can be done in numerous ways. At the very least membership of the appropriate professional organisation seems a basic starting point. Regardless of how well that organisation is run, it is difficult to claim professional status if one is not a member of the appropriate professional body. In addition the services supplied by that organisation, such as journals, conferences and other events, could be absolutely crucial in keeping up to date.

Regardless of how professionals keep their knowledge fresh, it is an ethical must that they do so unless they wish to risk their service to the customer suffering. The issues surrounding continuing professional development will be discussed in more detail in Chapter 7.

Conclusion

This chapter has sought to give some grounding in the key ethical issues facing librarians. The importance of ethics in librarianship cannot be overstated, and the chapters that follow will reinforce the issues discussed above in more detail.

Chapter 3 will discuss ethical codes from different parts of the world. Chapters 4 to 7 will discuss in more detail the key ethical issues facing librarians and present case studies to illustrate the points. Each case study will have a number of potential response choices, following which the implications of each choice for the librarian, the customer and the service will be discussed. Figure 2.2 highlights the model used for the case studies.

Figure 2.2   Case studies model

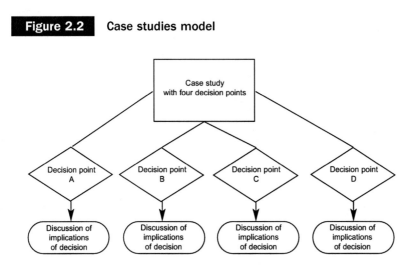

Ethical codes – an international overview

While LIS professionals may not operate under the same potential liabilities that other professionals such as doctors, dentists or lawyers have to consider, the issue of ethical practice should be of great concern to all in the profession. As Sturges notes, 'Although ethical dilemmas have a very high profile in medicine, and in some other professions such as law and financial services, they occur everywhere else that there is professional activity' (Sturges, 2002: 45). Indeed, while the chances of an ethical dilemma for a lawyer or a doctor being newsworthy has always been high, equally with the advent of universal Internet access in public libraries the chances of an ethical dilemma for librarians reaching the newspapers are also increasing. The newspapers seem to thrive on negative Internet stories, and such a case occurred in the Scottish city of Glasgow in 2001, when a newspaper journalist turned up in a branch library asking why a child had accessed pornography there. The subsequent furore even led to questions being asked in the Scottish Parliament about the incident, notwithstanding the coverage in the newspapers.

Professional associations by their very nature exist to represent the interests of their wider profession and to offer a guarantee to wider society that members of the profession all adhere to an agreed set of principles. In so doing, the formalising of a set of principles for association member behaviour becomes vital if the profession itself is to be afforded respect by those outside of the community. This is normally instigated by the formulation and development of an ethical code to which all professional association members are expected to conform.

This chapter will discuss the nature of some of the ethical codes within the LIS profession, and examine if different standards within different national associations can exist.

The need for ethical codes in professions

Ethical codes are useful documents for two specific reasons. Firstly they offer members of the professional association a model of behaviour that is expected of them. As observed by Koehler and Pemberton:

> Professional codes of ethics and formalized standards of practice are far more than window dressing or the mere expression of abstract, but unattainable principles. Ethical codes establish the parameters of acceptable behavior. They offer the practitioner a frame of reference to direct professional behavior. They also offer support and guidance for professionals where conflicts arise between the interests and demands of the profession and society as a whole or between their professional and corporate affiliations. (Koehler and Pemberton, 2000: 29)

Secondly they communicate a set of values to the wider world, including employers and other stakeholders. These are important points, and especially so in defining professional status for workers. If it is not clear what you stand for, it is a case of guesswork for people outside of the profession to know exactly what it is you do.

It is incredible that it took so long for many library associations to develop ethical codes. As mentioned in the previous chapter, the ALA was the first to develop a code in 1938, with European associations catching up much later. The next section of the chapter will discuss the nature of some of the ethical codes and highlight some of the differences that can be seen in emphasis depending on the region.

What the codes specify – an international overview

Based on their study of 37 separate ethical codes in our own discipline, Koehler and Pemberton identified six categories that most of the ethical codes covered, namely:

1. Client/patron rights and privileges
2. Selection issues
3. Professional practice

4. Access issues
5. Employer responsibility
6. Social issues. (Koehler and Pemberton, 2000: 34)

In this book we have arranged the case study themes around four categories:

1. Information – from selection to provision
2. Intellectual property issues
3. Issues of equity of access and privacy
4. Ethical management of the self, the individual and the organisation.

It is these four themes we will seek to identify within the ethical codes we discuss. A random selection of ethical codes will be discussed covering North America, Europe, Asia and Australasia. The rubric for selection will be that the associations discussed have placed their ethical code on the Internet and that it is current.

North American codes

American Library Association

http://www.ala.org/ala/oif/statementspols/codeofethics/codeethics.htm (ALA, 1995)

Ethical codes can be anything from full, detailed statements to small bullet point lists. We will start our discussion with an example of one of the more well-known ethical codes and the model for many others, that of the ALA. The code, last ratified in 1995, has eight separate strands, and begins with the emphasis on a broad overview of what members of the ALA provide, namely *the highest level of service to all library users through appropriate and usefully organized resources; equitable service policies; equitable access; and accurate, unbiased, and courteous responses to all requests.* This first statement covers a great deal of the library ethos in one sentence. From selection to provision, the ALA promotes high-quality customer service focused around equal access and unbiased information. The next section deals with censorship, stating that *We uphold the principles of intellectual freedom and resist all efforts to censor library resources.* Ensuring that the information provided to the user is free from influence on selection by outside parties is vital. Privacy and confidentiality are next, and the code states that *We protect each library user's right to privacy and confidentiality with respect to information sought or received and resources consulted, borrowed, acquired or transmitted.* This is an especially important goal in the modern era given the challenges to privacy in light of the legislation following 9/11.

Statement four is succinct: *We recognize and respect intellectual property rights.* Again this is a vital component of what librarians have done historically, but it offers major ethical challenges in a world where more people wish to download material free, and where rights holders increasingly become more draconian about the use of their intellectual property assets. Statement five relates to the ethical treatment of colleagues and employees: *We treat co-workers and other colleagues with respect, fairness and good faith, and advocate conditions of employment that safeguard the rights and welfare of all employees of our institutions.* The next statement returns to information selection and provision and focuses on ensuring that the librarian does not place private interests above those of the user or the employer: *We do not advance private interests at the expense of library users, colleagues, or our employing institutions.* Similarly, statement seven deals with the personal viewpoints of the librarian: *We distinguish between our personal convictions and professional duties and do not allow our personal beliefs to interfere with fair representation of the aims of our institutions or the provision of access to their information resources.* Both statements six and seven could be seen as covering dilemmas that are becoming increasingly prominent. The attempted influence of fundamentalists of all persuasions over the free flow of information and its selection is one of the major issues of the moment. Many religious organisations, for instance, seek to ensure that viewpoints that conflict or challenge their own are silenced, and in the area of creationism, or intelligent design, it could equally be the case that the librarian is a believer, or he or she is being pressured to stock materials by organisations that believe.

The final statement in the code states that *We strive for excellence in the profession by maintaining and enhancing our own knowledge and skills, by encouraging the professional development of co-workers, and by fostering the aspirations of potential members of the profession.* This specifically relates to the essential need of the librarian to remain up to date and to ensure that colleagues and any new entrants to the profession are made aware of the need to keep up to date. Essentially the statement relates to the needs to manage the self with as much concentration as the organisation.

As can be seen, the ALA Code attempts to cover very specific areas of a librarian's professional duties. As a model for ethical codes it is useful because it identifies the need for the librarian to concentrate not only on issues such as privacy, censorship and equity of access, but equally on professional development and ethical management. It is a broad-based code that attempts to consider the whole professional rather than only the librarian-specific body of knowledge.

Canadian Library Association

http://www.cla.ca/about/ethics.htm (CLA, 1976)

The Canadian Library Association (CLA) Code, developed in 1976, is a straightforward set of four numbered statements. The first statement requires members to *support and implement the principles and practices embodied in the current Canadian Library Association Statement on Intellectual Freedom.* This is interesting as it points to a larger policy statement, which in many ways states more about the ethical roles of members than the ethics code itself does (CLA, 1985). This distinct statement addresses issues related to equity of access, ensuring a broad coverage of materials and the need for librarians to guard against attacks on intellectual freedom. This statement then is an essential appendix to the ethical code.

The second statement of the ethical code states that members must *make every effort to promote and maintain the highest possible range and standards of library service to all segments of Canadian society.* The emphasis here is on diversity and quality of service. The next statement commits members to *facilitate access to any or all sources of information which may be of assistance to library users.* Again this statement relates to breadth of materials, but also user assistance in accessing those materials. The final statement combines the issues of treatment of staff and users, as it calls on members to *protect the privacy and dignity of library users and staff.* This relates to ethical management of staff members, but also to core privacy issues for users.

The CLA have taken a different approach to their ethical statement from that of the ALA, but we can see core issues of concern in both. Intellectual freedom and censorship, ethical treatment of users, privacy and ethical management are all topics which feature in both codes, and it will be interesting to see if these themes continue as we move to analyse European codes.

European codes

In analysing the European codes we will focus on one code ratified by a country that has had very little political instability, the UK, versus a code ratified by a former Eastern Bloc country that has recently become part of the European Union, the Czech Republic.

Chartered Institute of Library and Information Professionals

http://www.cilip.org.uk/professionalguidance/ethics (CILIP, 2005)

CILIP's ethical code is a long document which sets out in great detail the expectations of the professional association for its members' behaviour. Interestingly in the preamble it is reinforced that, while being a guiding set of principles, it is also the case that anyone in breach of the code could find themselves being subject to disciplinary action by the association:

> CILIP's Disciplinary Regulations provide that a Member will be guilty of professional misconduct if he/she has acted contrary to the aims, objects and interests of CILIP or in a manner unbecoming or prejudicial to the profession ... Members should therefore be aware that failure to comply with the Principles and Code may, depending on the circumstances, be a ground for disciplinary action.

Therefore CILIP's code has the potential to act as more than a mere mission statement of sorts: there are real potential problems for any librarian deemed to be in breach of the code.

The code itself is divided into several main parts: firstly a broad set of ethical principles followed by a code of professional practice, which itself is split into five sections. The ethical principles offer a generic list of twelve values, such as *Concern for the public good* and *Concern for the good reputation of the information profession*. These principles also include:

- impartiality, and avoidance of inappropriate bias, in acquiring and evaluating information and in mediating it to other information users;
- respect for confidentiality and privacy in dealing with information users;
- concern for the conservation and preservation of our information heritage in all formats;
- respect for, and understanding of, the integrity of information items and for the intellectual effort of those who created them;
- commitment to maintaining and improving personal professional knowledge, skills and competences.

The set of ethical principles, then, stand as a core set of values but they are not in any way proscriptive. Within the code of practice itself more detail is provided. The five sections of the code of practice are:

- Personal responsibilities
- Responsibilities to information and its users
- Responsibility to colleagues and the information community
- Responsibilities to society
- Responsibilities as employees.

Within these five sections a full set of sub-principles are described. Under *Personal responsibilities* the emphasis is on professional competency and professional development, although it also calls on members not to claim any expertise in an area they are not familiar with. In *Responsibilities to information and its users* the code discusses ensuring that the user is aware of the wide range of services on offer and that access to information is as straightforward as possible. Within this theme is also stressed the need to be impartial in selection of resources, the need to treat user queries with confidentiality and to ensure that any competing needs of information users are fairly dealt with. The responsibilities to information and users continue with emphasis on the balancing act of protecting the user's right to access versus the right of the creator of a work to legal and moral protection from abuse of their work. This section rounds off with a reminder of the librarian's role to preserve the knowledge of mankind for future generations.

Responsibility to colleagues and the information community promotes the notion of ethical behaviour towards colleagues, highlighting the need to encourage the development of the skills of both co-workers and employees. Interestingly, within this set of values aimed at promoting best practice in the service and in colleagues is a call to 'report significant breaches of this Code to the appropriate authorities'. This is an interesting point, as it puts the onus on members to ensure that they police their profession by reporting severe ethical breaches to CILIP.

Responsibilities to society emphasises the role of the librarian in promoting equitable access to information, and to continually work to ensure that the balance between access and protection of information resources is met. This section also calls on members to ensure that the ethical code is promoted both to colleagues and to society as a whole. *Responsibilities to employers* discusses the need for members to become engaged with the mission of the entire organisation and not just the library or information service. The need to ensure the organisation is operating ethically is also stressed, with a call to 'bring to the attention of their employer any concerns they may have concerning the ethics or legality of specific decisions, actions or behaviour at work.'

The CILIP code mirrors in many ways that of the ALA with its level of detail and proscription, but an interesting strand to CILIP's code is the repeated stress on members to ensure ethical practice not only in themselves but in others, even from the point of view of reporting unethical behaviour where they come across it.

Association of Library and Information Professionals of the Czech Republic

http://www.ifla.org/faife/ethics/czlacode.htm (IFLA, 2006a)

The code for Czech librarians was adopted in 2004. It mirrors the ALA and CILIP codes in its details, and it is not surprising to see an ex-Communist Bloc country emphasise the importance of democracy. The first statement calls on librarians to:

> always uphold the basic right of the individual to information. They provide for unlimited, equal, and free access to information and information sources in library collections. They do so irrespective of political, ideological and religious views and without any censorship, save for the exceptions stipulated by legislation. However, they bear no responsibility for the consequences of the use of information obtained from documents or in the library.

There is a lot encapsulated in this first statement, including the upholding of the free flow of information and the emphasis on political and religious censorship being challenged, but crucially the last part of the statement states that the librarian cannot be held accountable for the use to which a user puts the information. This is unusual in a code of ethics, as it attempts to place responsibility for information use on the user, a logical stance for an association wishing to protect its members from challenges of culpability. It is interesting to contrast this with Hauptman's 1976 experiment when he was seeking information on how to make a bomb, discussed earlier in the book.

The next part of the code focuses on accessibility of information. Members must *strive for broad accessibility of information contained in documents, regardless of the place of their storage.* The emphasis here may be on partnerships and reciprocal agreements, and that the physical location of an item should not be a barrier to access. The code continues by stating that members should *provide services to users irrespective of their nationality, race, religion, gender and social status.* This is a social statement relating to equity of access that is central to all of the codes so far discussed. Similarly, the code has an emphasis on intellectual property, also mirroring the codes so far discussed: members should *respect the rights of authors and treat their intellectual property in compliance with legislation.* This call, which suggests universal values for librarians, is echoed by a desire to respect the privacy of the user. The code calls on the librarian to *respect the rights of users to privacy and anonymity, basing their contact with them on respect for user personalities and information needs.* One can imagine such a call having even more resonance in a country where the right of privacy had been withdrawn for such a long period of time.

There follows another set of statements that would be equally at home in the ALA, CLA or CILIP Codes, and suggests that librarians:

- contribute through their professional performance and loyal conduct to the goodwill of the library;
- are aware of their affiliation to the professional community, respect colleagues from libraries of different types, keeping in close touch with them, and cooperate with colleagues from a wide network of memory institutions;
- keep themselves well-informed with developments in their profession, striving for life-long education and professional advancement;
- support with words and deeds those colleagues who have found

themselves in difficulties due to their observance of the principles of this Code of Ethics.

The emphasis here is on professional competency based around networking, and continuing professional development.

The Czech code is an interesting set of values, mirroring much of the western codes we have so far discussed. We move now to a discussion of some Asian codes.

Asian codes

In the discussion of codes from Asian library associations we will focus on two countries, firstly Indonesia and then the Philippines.

Indonesia

http://www.ifla.org/faife/ethics/ipicode.htm (IFLA, 2006b)

Indonesia is a predominantly Muslim country where the religion has a large role in culture and politics. This is reflected in the ethical code of the Association for Indonesian Librarians. The code is divided into three chapters, with Chapter One defining the role of a librarian:

> The librarian is an individual, who carries out the activities of the library's functions, documentation and information, by giving service to the society according to the range of duty of the main organisation, based on his/her own knowledge of library, documentation and information science obtained through the education. [*sic*]

This is a straightforward definition that could describe a librarian in any country on the globe. Chapter Two of the code specifies common duties for librarians which are as follows:

1. Every Indonesian librarian should be fully aware that the profession of librarians is a profession, which mainly carries out educational tasks and research.
2. Every Indonesian librarian in performing their profession should care for dignity and moral and give priority to obey the nation and the country.

3. Every Indonesian librarian must appreciate and love Indonesian identity and culture.
4. Every Indonesian librarian use his/her knowledge for the benefit of human fellowship, society, nation and religion.
5. Every Indonesian librarian should respect the secrecy of the information of personal character, received from servicing the society.

As a set of principles this certainly seems different from those codes discussed above. There is more emphasis here on the state and religion than we have seen so far, and it would be doubtful if these values would be seen in the codes of the ALA, CLA or CILIP. Point five mirrors the emphasis of the other codes we have discussed in relation to privacy of personal data, however. There is obviously a much clearer emphasis here on the librarian's responsibility to society and the home country. Point two, relating to obeying the nation and country, is certainly something that many western librarians may find problematic. Equally as problematic for western librarians is the notion emphasising that a librarian should benefit the religion. In a multi-cultural society such a call would be dangerous and risk other religions being marginalised. Yet in a single-faith state, is such a call as problematic?

Chapter Three relates to the librarian's duty to the professional organisation and the wider profession. It defines these duties as follows:

1. To upgrade science profession development among librarians, every Indonesian librarian should make the Association of Indonesian Librarians a forum for cooperation, a place for consultation, and a place for personal training.
2. For the interest of science development and of librarians in Indonesia, every Indonesian librarian should contribute with energy, thought and funds to the organisation.
3. By holding high the good name of the Association of Indonesian Librarians, every Indonesian librarian should keep away from all acts, expressions and attitudes, which could damage the organisation and the profession.

The emphasis here is on duty and loyalty to the image of the association and the profession. Mirroring the other codes we have discussed we see a continuing emphasis on professional development.

Philippines

http://www.ifla.org/faife/ethics/filicode.htm (IFLA, 2006c)

We move now to a discussion of the code for librarians from the Philippines, otherwise known as the *Professional Regulation Commission of the Republic of the Philippines – Code of Ethics for Registered Librarians.* This is a large code, divided into six articles with 31 separate statements. We will not discuss all of them in this chapter, but instead highlight some of the more interesting.

Article One relates to the librarian's relationship with society. It calls on the librarian to *recognize and respect the supreme authority of the State as expressed through its laws and implemented by its agencies.* It also calls for librarians to *always observe that the well-being of the public and interest of the State are above the well-being and interest of any individual.* Interestingly, and similar to the Indonesian code, we see an emphasis on the duty to the state. As a starting point, again, this differs from the western codes we have discussed, which emphasise wider society above the state. It is possible, for instance, to see occasions where the duty to the state may put one in conflict with a duty to the wider society.

Article Two relates to relationships with clients. A great deal of this mirrors the codes we have previously seen, with an emphasis on *the highest level of service through courteous, prompt, adequate, skilful, accurate and unbiased responses to all requests for assistance* and the essential need not to *discriminate against any library user.* Article Three relates to the relationship of the librarian with the wider profession and colleagues, emphasising the duty of the librarian to the promotion and integrity of librarianship. This article contains statements relating to personal interests, impartiality, continuing professional development and freedom of expression. Again we see here a set of values that are repeated in the other codes we have discussed, suggesting a universality of professional duty across continents.

Article Five relates to the librarian's duty to the organisation, and here we see an emphasis on developing and protecting library systems, guarding against censorship and acting in good faith. Article Five relates to the librarian's duty to themselves, focusing on issues such as the accepting of gifts to influence purchasing decisions, the avoidance of conflict of interest and the necessity to ensure that professional time and effort is appropriately recompensed. The final article merely relates to the implementation of the code.

The ethical code for the Philippines is an extremely interesting document. It offers such proscription in its suggestions, but in all it is governed by the absolute highest standards of accountability and service. While the cultural issues related to both it and the Indonesian codes sees an emphasis on the state, and in the case of Indonesia also religion, both documents offer a broad set of ethical values that mirror many of the western codes. In the preamble of the Filipino code it states:

> Librarians are imbued with lofty ideals of service to people through books and other records of knowledge, a service they believe is their best way to serve humanity, enrich people's lives and attain self actualization.

Such ideals are universal in nature and offer the notion that the ethical values of librarians are the same regardless of the continent in which the librarian practices.

Australasian codes

For the Australasian codes under discussion we will focus on those for librarians from Australia and New Zealand.

Australia

http://www.alia.org.au/policies/professional.conduct.html (ALIA, 2005)

The guiding principle behind the Australian Library and Information Association's (ALIA) *Statement on Professional Conduct* is that *People engaged in library and information services are members of a profession committed to intellectual freedom and the free flow of ideas and information.* The statement then goes on to list seven key principles to which librarians should adhere.

These principles make it the responsibility of the librarian to encourage 'intellectual freedom and the free flow of information and ideas'. Again the focus is on the freedom to express one's views and for that to spread throughout society. The emphasis then is on the need for the librarian to perform their duties professionally, 'exercising their responsibilities within the context of duty of care for the clients of the library and information services they offer'. Intellectual property then is the focus, with again the emphasis on respect for other people's creative works. This is followed by a focus on the privacy and confidentiality of the user.

An interesting point in the ALIA code is the call for the librarian to distinguish *in their actions and statements between their personal viewpoints and those of the library and information service that employs them or the Australian Library and Information Association.* This reminds librarians of their responsibility to the organisation and the professional body, and not to assume that anything said or done while working as a librarian is automatically subject to defence by the profession. The last two statements follow familiar paths, with an emphasis on continuing professional development and the need to ensure that one avoids conflicts of interest.

New Zealand

http://www.ifla.org/faife/ethics/nzcode.htm (IFLA, 2006d)

The code of the Library and Information Association of New Zealand Aotearoa (LIANZA) is similar in style to that of its neighbour, ALIA. It too has seven points, the first focusing on the librarian's duty to the user and to society by assisting *in the collection, preservation and availability of recorded and transmitted knowledge and ideas* and by facilitating *the flow of information and ideas.*

The code then suggests that all *Librarians' actions and decisions should be based firmly on sound professional practice.* This statement emphasises the importance of a professional body of knowledge to ethical practice.

The next point relates to discrimination, and urges librarians when providing services not to discriminate *on the grounds of socio-economic status, politics, race, colour, creed, gender or sexual orientation.* Point four relates to the privacy of the individual and highlights the importance of ensuring that user data is secure and professionally managed. Point five reminds librarians of the need to continuously update professional skills, keeping *abreast of new developments and applications in their particular areas of professional activity.* The final two points relate to ethical management, firstly highlighting the need to ensure that librarians *should not profit from their positions save by normal remuneration nor should they have any financial interest in goods or services recommended or supplied without first disclosing that interest.* The final point relates to the development of library policies, and to their ethical development and implementation.

Conclusion

From the eight codes discussed in this chapter we can see a pattern of interests that represent a global set of ethical concerns for librarians. Consistent emphasis was related to:

- concerns over censorship and user privacy;
- focus on intellectual freedom and freedom of expression;
- adherence to intellectual property legislation;
- commitment to professional development;
- focus on ethical behaviour.

Koehler and Pemberton in their much wider study of 37 ethical codes concluded that there are certain intrinsic values within ethical codes from different countries that could be filtered and used to propose a model code. These included focusing on the needs of clients, understanding the nature of your professional role, supporting the profession and the professional association, being sensitive to your social responsibilities, and being aware of the rights of users, employers, other librarians, your community and wider society (Koehler and Pemberton, 2000: 39).

While codes from different associations may vary in their length and their level of proscription, they offer a very similar core set of values for the practice of librarianship. In this discussion of ethical codes we have highlighted some of these key values that are cherished by library associations the world over. The chapters that follow will discuss many of these issues in more detail and offer case studies to highlight the range of ethical choices that can be made for many scenarios. At the heart of each case study will be the pressure to decide what is right based on the ethical concerns of the user, the profession, the employer and wider society.

4

The ethics of information supply – from selection to provision

'I am looking for scientific evidence that proves the existence of the Loch Ness Monster.'

The cycle of supplying information to a user is a tried and tested one. From the initial selection, purchase, classification and cataloguing, and processing for public use to final exploitation by the user, the system has not altered a great deal over the decades and centuries librarians have been undertaking this task. Each stage of the process presents its own set of challenges from an ethical point of view.

Selection

Selection of material can be one of the most controversial aspects of librarianship. Ultimately the goal is to select appropriate materials on behalf of users, not merely to satisfy current needs but to attempt to anticipate future needs too. The controversies that can occur in the selection process are varied, but ensuring the material purchased is appropriate for the user groups served by the library is absolutely vital.

In public libraries and academic libraries it is often common to find subject specialists who are charged with the responsibility for ensuring a broad coverage of materials in a specific area. This normally means that the individual charged with purchasing for subject ranges can build up a thorough knowledge of the areas concerned and, equally importantly, an idea of the library's coverage in those areas. It is important when one is charged with the role of developing specific subject collections that personal prejudices do not come into the selection of materials. For instance, a wide knowledge of an area may mean that particular authors are favoured over others, which might be a quite legitimate stance from the point of view of current thought on a topic. However, a library should represent a broad opinion of materials on a topic, and balance is important, whether the librarian agrees with the authors or not.

Similarly the selection of fiction titles can be a problematic issue, especially in public and school libraries. Cultural pressures to purchase material that is 'worthy' as opposed to popular can often be felt. The unethical way to handle this is to only purchase material that the library patrons do not want; ultimately the librarian can use reader development initiatives to attempt to guide readers towards other titles that may enhance or stretch their reading skills, but to assume they will borrow tougher titles because their favourites are no longer stocked is as foolhardy as it is unethical. On the issue of reader development and book promotion in general, it is often the case that publishers or book vendors can sponsor initiatives within libraries to promote books by specific authors or on specific themes. These are often highly valued by customers, but the librarian needs to be careful that the materials being promoted are titles that they would have sanctioned had they been chosen by them and not promoted by the publisher. It should be remembered that something as positive as a sponsored event can chip away at professional ethics if the librarian is compromising at all on any of the titles promoted. Such events should be broadly welcomed, but the librarian should always have a key role in deciding which titles are promoted to their customers, and there should never be a scenario that sees a librarian compromising his or her professional judgement on the appropriateness of the titles promoted just to gain the sponsored event for their library. This is a slippery slope that ultimately leaves the customer with no independent filter for the materials they are supplied with. Indeed Badaracco (2002) asks the question, is book publicity ever morally neutral? The logicality of librarians having close links with publishers is obvious, but while the ethical questions related to such relationships may be buried a little deep in the collective subconscious of librarianship, they remain questions all the same.

Similarly the personal or religious beliefs of a librarian should never interfere with or influence the selection criteria applied. Fundamental to the selection process should be a clear understanding of the community served and their needs, and even though this may mean providing materials that offend the librarian's personal sensibilities, the librarian should never allow personal beliefs to influence this process.

Purchasing

Controversies around purchasing tend to focus on appropriate use of resources. This can be from the point of view of ensuring that the organisation and thus the user get the best value for money from vendors, often involving tendering processes for business. Secondly, the professional must ensure that the relationship with any vendor is not influenced by anything other than value for money. In other words the selection of vendors must be above board and not based on favours or discrimination of one over another on anything other than value for money or service grounds. This also ensures that purchasing relationships with vendors are cost-effective. Library supply is very big business, and librarians with responsibility for purchasing should always ensure that relationships with company representatives are properly conducted and that no incentives are involved when contracts are awarded.

The recent growth in supplier selection of material is also a potential ethical issue that needs to be considered. In the UK the government is keen for the public and private sectors to work more in collaboration with each other, not merely in libraries but across government services. This has seen a pressure in public libraries to outsource services like supply of books. A 2005 report authored by a firm of accountants for the Museums, Libraries and Archives section of the Department for Culture, Media and Sport of the UK government acknowledged that:

> It has been argued that local selection of books is important to ensure that a library meets the requirements of the local community and in some cases to ensure that users have a say in book selection. Book selection by suppliers may be controversial but it works in some places already. (DCMS, 2005)

Certainly research may well suggest that supplier selection is effective *in some cases*, but the notion that it is *better* than local librarians selecting for their customers is difficult to prove. More worryingly from the point of view of professional librarianship is that it takes away one of the vital roles of the librarian in the information chain. While the material selected can quite conceivably be based on previous statistics and preferences, removing the local dimension could be problematic on several fronts. The report also suggests that commercial suppliers should have access to library management system data on borrowings, which has the potential to open up questions of privacy. Again librarians need to ensure that such fundamental changes being made to the working processes are based on evidence rather than political motivation. It may well be the case that the librarian has no say in this, but they should be aware of the ethical concerns inherent in the changes, and they should be acutely aware of the potential damage such notions may do to their professional status. It seems churlish on the one hand for librarians to campaign on issues such as privacy and rights to anonymity, when we may be prepared to give outside bodies access to the same data for purchasing decisions on our behalf.

Cataloguing and classification

This may seem an unlikely area for ethical reflection: however, there are issues that should be considered. One of the first tools a user may employ to find information is the library catalogue. To make the catalogue as accessible as possible the challenge for the cataloguer is to ensure an item is classified and catalogued appropriately, but this does not always mean to the absolute standard available. For example, many public libraries use a simplified form of the Dewey Decimal classification designed to make books easy to find. The ethical decision being made here is that it is better to make resources accessible than to meet exacting cataloguing standards that may see a book with ten or so numbers after the point. As an example of this and another issue which can arise, a book on Scottish Law as it relates to the mentally handicapped has two copies available within the libraries of a Scottish library service, one copy in a reference library, one in a community library. The classifications are below:

- 346.0138 – community library
- 344.1106138 – reference library

A university library in the same city classified the same title under the following number:

- 348.075252

And in another university library in a different city:

- 344.41044

While the cataloguers' decisions may not at first glance be seen to be ethical concerns, they are in as much as they have used their professional judgement to arrange an item within their library. Obviously as long as all materials that are similar are similarly catalogued and classified within the same library then there is no major issue here, but the arrangement of the title places the item within that library's organisation of the collected knowledge it stores. Its placement within that structure has ethical implications.

Consider, for example, the controversy over intelligent design and creationism versus evolution, an ongoing ethical issue for many librarians, especially in North America. Again depending on your ethical viewpoint, you may see intelligent design as a logical explanation for how the planet evolved or as an attempt to dress theology in a scientific cloak. Yet the placement of books on intelligent design on the shelves beside science books has raised a furore in American schools. Several school districts in the USA required that intelligent design, a form of creationism that counters evolutionary theory and suggests that intelligence was involved in the creation of the world and of man, be presented in science classes as an alternative scientific theory to evolution. In the Dover School District of Pennsylvania it was a requirement in ninth grade science classes that a statement be read to pupils suggesting that although the class was being taught evolution it was only one theory and that intelligent design was another plausible theory. In other school districts it was a requirement that the librarian place notices in all science books dealing with evolution that said much the same thing as the Dover statement. Eleven parents filed suit against the school district in Dover and in late December 2005 the courts ruled in their favour and pronounced that the teaching of intelligent design in schools was unconstitutional. Librarians in the USA have been wrestling with this controversy for several years. In the Dover case 60 copies of a textbook on intelligent design were donated to the school libraries and the librarian was instructed by the School Superintendent to place them on the shelves (O'Sullivan and O'Sullivan, 2005). To be pressured into classifying an item as a science text when the librarian knows it is a religious text is a serious ethical dilemma for a librarian, yet this is what has happened in the recent past in the world's largest democracy. The influence of religious groups will be revisited in other areas of this book, but at this stage it is appropriate to note that the intelligent design controversy is only one area where religious groups are challenging the professional ethics of librarians. A 2002 work edited by Gregory A. Smith sought to consider how librarians who are Christians reconcile their beliefs with their profession and raises many of these issues (Smith, 2002).

On the subject of classification, the Dewey Decimal system itself could be discussed as an ethical case in point. The structure devised by Dewey reflects his original vision of how the knowledge of the world should be arranged. It is a consciously pro-western and pro-Christian way to organise the collected works of mankind, and while it works exceedingly well, the arrangement could very well be seen to reinforce old stereotypes of how the West views the rest of the world. Consider again the thorny topic of religion for a moment. In the Dewey system Christianity occupies a large swathe of the available categories for Religion, the 200s. The ranges from 201 to 289 are predominantly concerned with Christianity and the rest of the world's religions are squeezed into 290–299. While not questioning the efficiency of this system, the ethical viewpoint it is promoting is one that reduces the religions of the majority of mankind into one tenth of the space available in the system. This is potentially offensive to many, and while it will not have been the intention of Melvil Dewey to offend, the potential for the system to do so should always be noted. How we organise the knowledge we are making available to our users is of crucial concern from an ethical standpoint.

Delivery of information

Delivering information to users is perhaps the most important aspect of a library's service. Librarianship is a people profession and all of the back-office work of ordering, selecting and organising would be for nothing if there was not a user group at the end of the chain to take advantage of the work. Ethical issues related to delivery of information can be broken down into the following categories:

- ensuring material is appropriate for a user;
- ensuring material is reliable.

Deciding on the appropriateness of material can be a tricky ethical issue and can easily segue into censorship if handled improperly. It is vital then that librarians know their client group and put systems in place to ensure that the material gets to those who need it while ensuring that those who should not access it do not. A common example of this is in public libraries. There are many books and resources that, while being perfectly appropriate for adults, are not so for children or young people. This can be handled simply by use of categories on a library management system (LMS). Books or other resources that are catalogued as being inappropriate for young people will automatically be unavailable if a person under a specific age attempts to borrow them. The process normally involves an error message appearing on the screen of the LMS if a member without the right to access the resource attempts to borrow it. The need to handle this at LMS level becomes important because the library staff will not necessarily be able to determine whether a book is inappropriate for an age group unless it has already been evaluated. This could be for several reasons: the staff members issuing books at the counter may be paraprofessional staff or other staff members not involved in the selection or cataloguing and classification of material. Secondly, they may simply not be familiar with the resource or have time on a busy counter to evaluate it quickly. In large public library systems this evaluation is normally conducted centrally in order that every library stocking the book or resource treats it in exactly the same way.

Despite the common process cited above, controversy can remain even when a book has been evaluated as being appropriate for young people. In the USA the American Library Association (ALA) has an annual banned books week which takes place every September. Its goal is to highlight the level of attempted censorship in public and school libraries across America and in March 2006 the ALA reported there were 405 attempts to ban books from libraries (ALA, 2006). It is common (and perhaps predictable) to see titles in the list that have for their subject matter issues such as teenage sexuality and issues regarding race and ethnicity. However, when such revered books as *Huckleberry Finn* and *Of Mice and Men* are among the list of challenged titles it can clearly be seen what the dangers are of not taking on the challenge of fighting for free speech and availability of creative works. The ALA and other professional library associations play a vital role in advocacy here, campaigning for the right of library customers to access materials regardless of how controversial they are. This advocacy role has become all the more important as in recent years pressure groups have become much more vociferous in their campaigning. These controversies are invariably built around religious groups attempting to ban materials, and in sheer weight of numbers their voices are growing louder and beginning to have an effect. The recent controversy over the cartoons of Mohammed published by a Danish newspaper is a case in point. In theory libraries stocking the newspapers concerned could have been seen as a legitimate target for protest, as they were in the early 1990s in the UK when Salman Rushdie's *The Satanic Verses* was deemed by some

Muslims as blasphemous. Sensitivities being what they currently are in the early twenty-first century, it would be easy to give into pressure and remove an item from the library shelves, but the logical conclusion of that is a world where free speech is at the exigency of whichever pressure group shouts loudest. Even in the West it is a mistake to assume that politicians will fight for free speech, and occasionally they need to be reminded of their responsibilities by professional associations. It is a core role for librarians to campaign vigorously for free speech and counter any attempt at censorship of the materials they make available for their customers.

This takes us to the issue of reliability of information. In the past librarians selected the information they provided from the published works of the world. This tended to mean that most published works had some provenance to them, and certainly from the point of view of reference works a canon developed over the decades. Trusted sources were easy to identify as they normally produced a core set of materials available in most libraries. The advent of the Internet has meant that anyone anywhere can publish, and while this is ultimately democratic it is also dangerous. The increasing popularity of materials such as Wikipedia places us in an entirely new area from the point of view of encyclopaedic information. While its collective focus is an interesting model for the future, the occasional but highly public instances of vandalism to the information stored there pose serious questions for librarians who recommend the source to customers. How can you be sure that the information on their site is completely accurate? Obviously the key task is to ensure that customers are reminded to confirm the information they find with other sources, but rather worryingly the public increasingly relies on single sources for information. In the classes we teach, for instance, we have seen a huge growth in the number of students citing Wikipedia as references for essay work without confirming the facts in other public sources, even when they are as freely available to them as Wikipedia. Even the Googleisation of society should be a concern for librarians. Reliance on one source for information needs is ultimately dangerous, especially when such a source is commercial in origin. The question that follows the title to this chapter, 'I am looking for scientific evidence that proves the existence of the Loch Ness Monster', may seem frivolous. In the era before the Internet such a question would have been answered from the point of view of published resources on the topic, books chosen by librarians. In the Internet age there will be many sites that offer 'evidence' for those who wish to believe it on any topic. Has the librarian to guide a customer to such a site with no comment on efficacy or reliability? The ethical dilemma here is a challenging one, since if the belief system held by the customer seems strange or even silly to the librarian, it may still be a belief system held strongly. The customer may not wish to hear that there is no Loch Ness Monster and that any site claiming there is should be approached critically.

Regardless of the belief system a person may have, there is a source of information on it available on the Internet. This is as true for extreme belief systems as it is for mainstream ones, which on the one hand is a positive thing as it can bring like minded people together, but on the other hand it can be negative if the belief system concerned is ludicrous, extreme or potentially dangerous to society. The emphasis here has to be on increasing information literacy instruction, even when customers do not think they require it. Indeed, how ethical would it be to allow a customer to leave a library knowing that the site he or she accessed and the information subsequently found on it is unreliable or, worse, completely false? In August 2006 a programme aired in the UK entitled *My Child Is Psychic*. In one scene a mother was seen sitting at a public library Internet terminal looking up sites on her son's health. Her son had extremely high brain activity diagnosed by doctors, and the parent found sites that suggested his high brain activity was a sign that he was psychic. This then led the mother to seek out alternative treatment for her son from someone who shared this belief. That someone can use a public library to access such information is obviously a new development and should worry librarians. Certainly in the days before the Internet, it is hard to envisage a scenario such as the above.

Delivery of information to users is one of the most vital aspects of a librarian's role. The ethics inherent in the decision-making are fundamental to our professional ethos and our role in supporting society's positive and life-enhancing use of information. Getting it wrong may well be professionally unethical, but it could also be potentially dangerous for the individual librarian and the organisation. Hannabuss discusses the topic of negligence and subsequent liability in a 2000 paper, and he raises a number of pertinent questions. Firstly, is supplying an inaccurate piece of information to a customer a form of negligence? If so, does that mean there may be potential liability for providing an inaccurate service (Hannabuss, 2000: 317)? In the world of commercial information one could see just such a scenario, yet there is no reason to assume that the public world of librarianship should operate to any less stringent a level. Indeed our professional pride should not tolerate such a reduction in standards as to assume that passing on inaccurate information is just one of those things. We live in an increasingly litigious world, and it is not outwith the realms of possibility that the provision of inaccurate information could have a negative impact on a customer. How they then react to that potential setback is in the lap of the gods, and may well see the librarian or their employer in the courts.

To summarise, then, the supply chain of information from purchasing to customer use is a crucial set of processes for the professional librarian. Each stage involves its own ethical questions that need to be understood and addressed if ethical practice is to be maintained. The case studies that follow will attempt to illustrate a range of these ethical questions.

Case studies

Case study 4.1 Looking a gift horse in the mouth

Marjorie Faye is the librarian in a school library in the US State of Georgia. The library she operates serves a student body of around 800 teenagers. One day a parcel arrives from a local church group. On opening the parcel Marjorie finds 20 copies of a textbook which discusses the science of evolution. On closer inspection she notices that the books have been authored by an organisation that promotes the intelligent design theory as an alternative to evolution. Marjorie is concerned about placing the material on the library shelves, but makes an appointment with the Principal to discuss the donation and the school's response to it.

At the meeting Marjorie discovers that the church group has already written to the Principal to let them know about the donation. The letter states that it hopes the school will find space on the library shelves for the textbooks. The Principal suggests that as the local church group has a number of representatives on the local school board any refusal to place the book in the library might lead to an uncomfortable monthly board meeting. Marjorie expresses her concerns that placing the book on the shelf beside the other books on evolution brings religion into the school system, and more importantly gives religion a place on the library shelves beside science.

The Principal acknowledges Marjorie's concerns but suggests the pragmatic approach would be to place some of the textbooks on the library shelves.

Which of the following decisions should Marjorie take?

A Marjorie agrees that the pragmatic approach is to place the books on the library shelves. She returns to the library and begins to process the books in order that they are available for the students later that day.
   Go to section A4.1

B Marjorie agrees to add the books to the library, but only if they can be classified as religious textbooks and not science textbooks.
   Go to section B4.1

C Marjorie attempts to convince the Principal that even the pragmatic approach she suggests is not appropriate, as it opens the floodgates for other groups to have questionable material placed on the shelves. She suggests the Principal stands firm in the face of any objections.
   Go to section C4.1

D Marjorie refuses to place the material on the library shelves and tells the Principal she believes the request insults her professional ethics and would be a disservice to the students.
   Go to section D4.1

Case study 4.2 Misinformation highway

Jane Leishman is the community librarian in a public library that services a small inner-city community. While tidying up uncollected printouts from the computers one afternoon, she finds a page from a health website that discusses curing cancer with positive thinking and meditation. Another member of staff passes and discusses with Jane the nature of the printout. She tells Jane that she assumes the copy must be an extra copy as the patron concerned had asked for information on websites that offered alternative treatments for late-stage cancer and she had suggested this one after using Google and seeing the testimonials on the website. The member of staff is someone Jane has always known to have interest in alternative and new age beliefs, but she had never considered her beliefs would be promoted on the job, especially for such an important issue and such a potentially vulnerable customer.

On further discussing the case with the member of staff, Jane also discovers that the patron was shown sites on curing disease with crystals, and the member of staff recommended a local store that sold new age and alternative health remedies.

As the person in charge of the community library Jane is ultimately responsible for the quality of service provided by her staff. Jane is very concerned that information on such unproven methods has been supplied to a vulnerable customer, and ponders how she could potentially remedy the situation, both in terms of ensuring staff know their ethical roles and in terms of ensuring the patron understands that the information supplied may be of limited value.

Which of the following decisions should Jane take?

A Jane decides that the member of staff concerned needs to be disciplined for allowing her personal beliefs to intrude into the job. The decision to do so greatly upsets the rest of the staff, as the member being disciplined is highly popular and the staff cannot see why Jane is being so heavy-handed when all the member of staff did was attempt to help someone.

    Go to section A4.2

B Jane feels that she needs to attempt to track down the patron and ensure she is told that the information supplied to her is not reliable. The member of staff concerned is upset by this suggested approach as it insults her personal beliefs and calls into question her competence. Jane attempts to explain to the member of staff why a publicly funded body needs to avoid handing out information from websites that have no provenance, regardless of how convincing the information is.

    Go to section B4.2

C Jane develops an information literacy session for all staff in the community library ensuring that when working with customers they point out the dangers of relying on web-based information from unreliable sources. In addition she invests in poster material that reinforces the message regarding the mixed quality of information on the Web.

    Go to section C4.2

D Jane decides to implement a new policy ensuring that no information request should be responded to unless it is cleared by her or another senior member of staff. She understands that this will bring a higher workload and in the short term may be hard to manage, but feels that she needs to see all pieces of information supplied to customers until she can be assured of the competence of the staff members.

    Go to section D4.2

Case study 4.3 Who's promoting whom?

Artur Zurawski is the Adult Services Librarian with responsibility for reader development and book promotion for a library region that covers eight community libraries. The Library Director approaches Artur with a proposal for a book promotion initiative that will encompass all eight libraries in the area. The initiative would consist of promoting three authors who are all contracted to one publisher. Ten copies of all titles by each author will be made available to each community library, with appropriate marketing materials included such as posters and bookmarks. The libraries will receive copies of all books at 50 per cent discount.

Artur is generally positive about the idea, although he is concerned that he is unfamiliar with any of the authors in question or the publisher. In passing some colleagues mention to Artur that the publishing company involved is actually owned by a friend of the Library Director. On investigating further Artur begins to have major doubts about the quality of the work the libraries will be promoting. He discovers that the publisher is actually a vanity publisher (charging authors for publication of their work) and he decides to discuss his serious concerns with the Director.

The Director suggests to Artur that the decision has already been made and that Artur should just keep his concerns to himself and implement the project. The Director argues that since the publishing company is local it is the duty of the library service to promote them. Artur suggests that the material being promoted is of questionable quality, a point on which the Director disagrees.

Which of the following decisions should Artur take?

A Artur carries out the instructions of the Library Director and implements the project to the full extent of his skills. He encourages the eight libraries to promote the material to customers in order to achieve maximum issues. He also ensures that feedback from customers is recorded as to their experiences and enjoyment of the books in order to offer a full and accurate evaluative report to the Library Director at the completion of the project.
  Go to section A4.3

B Artur carries out the instructions of the Library Director, but gives the project very little of his attention and does not encourage the libraries involved to market the material to customers. His hope is that the project is unsuccessful and thus the Library Director will not be able to justify the project to the Library Board.

Go to section B4.3

C Artur suggests a compromise to the Library Director that the library staff work with the publisher but are allowed to select the books they think will be best for their customers. Artur's belief is that it would at least allow some form of quality control to be introduced into the project. He also suggests to the Library Director that the project emphasis could be changed to incorporate creative writing workshops and that the books be used as one example of how aspiring writers can get published.

Go to section C4.3

D Artur refuses to participate in the project suggesting that to promote material of such questionable quality is an insult to both staff and customers. He suggests that such projects should be decided upon by a group of library staff rather than just the Director, and that where there are any conflicts of interest the member of staff concerned could remove themselves from the decision-making process. The Director's reaction to this is to threaten disciplinary action against Artur unless he carries out the instructions.

Go to section D4.3

Case study 4.4 An issue of refusal to issue!

Grace Nakamura is a library assistant in a small community library. One morning a teenage boy comes to the counter with a DVD to borrow. The DVD is from the adult selection and has a certification that states it should only be viewed by people over the age of 18 and thus the library management system (LMS) will not allow the item to be leant to a teenage library card holder. Grace politely informs the teenager that she is unable to issue the DVD, and the teenager leaves the library in an unhappy state.

Around 30 minutes later the teenager returns with his mother. The mother asks to speak to the member of staff who would not issue the DVD to their son. Grace talks to the parent and explains her reasons for not lending the item to the boy, to which the parent replies it is not the business of the library what her son is allowed to watch. Grace informs the mother that it is when it comes to breaching library regulations, and that the LMS would simply not allow the item to be leant to her son. The mother then produced her own library card and tells her son to go and get the DVD he wanted and she would borrow it for him.

Grace reinforces to the mother that the DVD is not suitable for her son, to which the mother replies that she should mind her own business.

Which of the following options should Grace take?

A Grace attempts to continue to argue the case for the mother not showing the film to her son. Despite this the mother becomes increasingly irate and demands that she be allowed to borrow the DVD. Grace reluctantly issues the DVD to the mother's library ticket, and the mother and son leave the library.

  Go to section A4.4

B Grace calls for the senior member of staff on duty to discuss the situation with the mother. The senior member of staff reinforces what Grace has told her, but the mother insists that she will be borrowing the DVD and whether or not she allows her son to watch it is between her and her son. The senior member of staff on duty reluctantly issues the item to the mother, and she and the son leave the library.

  Go to section B4.4

C Grace refuses to issue the DVD to the mother, insisting that it would be improper for her to do so in the knowledge that she would be allowing her son to view the material. This makes the mother extremely angry and the debate between the two becomes heated. The mother insists on speaking to the person in charge to make a formal complaint against Grace.

  Go to section C4.4

D Grace is adamant in her own mind that she will not issue the DVD to the mother on a point of principle. She pretends to attempt to issue the item to the mother's card only to tell her that the LMS is showing that there is in fact a prior reservation on the system for that title and that she cannot issue the item at that time. The mother becomes angry and suggests that Grace is misleading her because she does not want to issue the item to her, and she insists on speaking to Grace's supervisor to make a complaint.

  Go to section D4.4

Case study discussions

Sections A4.1 – A4.4

A4.1 Looking a gift horse in the mouth

Marjorie's decision to support the Principal is problematic for several reasons. Firstly, the separation of church and state is enshrined in US law and as such the decision to place religious textbooks on the shelves in the guise of science textbooks could be illegal. Secondly, the decision means that other interest groups may well see the school as an easy touch to send their questionable material to be placed on the shelves. It will be harder to argue not to take the texts of other interest groups with this decision.

A4.2 Misinformation highway

Deciding to discipline the member of staff raises a number of issues for Jane. Firstly, if the member of staff did not realise what she was doing was wrong then the fundamental issue is not the member of staff, but the quality of training the staff have received. As the person responsible for the services provided by the library, Jane should take ultimate responsibility for any problems arising from the information supplied. It is her duty to ensure the staff she is responsible for have the tools necessary for the job. In addition the decision to discipline has unsettled staff, to whom the decision may look like passing the buck.

A4.3 Who's promoting whom?

Carrying out the project in a professional manner and ensuring that it is properly evaluated seems a pragmatic approach, and it would at least offer independent evidence as to whether or not the project was successful or not. Artur may feel that he has been undermined by being forced to carry out the project against his wishes, but if his belief is that the material is of low quality then it is highly likely that proper evaluation of the project will reflect this. The issue of the conflict of interest faced by the Library Director in implementing the programme in the first place is not an issue that directly influences front-line services, and thus for Artur to allow this to impact on his ability to deliver for the customer would be inappropriate. At the project's end Artur could revisit his concerns and may have evidence in hand to demonstrate that the

Library Director demonstrated an error of judgement in proceeding with the initiative.

A4.4 An issue of refusal to issue!

Grace could be seen to be doing the right thing by attempting to persuade the mother that borrowing the DVD to show it to her son is inappropriate, but ultimately she may have to concede defeat and lend the item to the mother. This may be different if any rule exists in the library regulations that allows staff to withhold an item if they believe it will be viewed by a minor, but assuming in this case that this rule does not exist, Grace can feel she has attempted to do the ethical thing by pointing out to mother that the DVD is for adults only.

Sections B4.1 – B4.4

B4.1 Looking a gift horse in the mouth

Marjorie's suggestion that the books could be placed on the shelves but deliberately placed with the religious textbooks and not the science textbooks seems a sensible compromise on the one hand. However, it means that material of questionable scientific merit remains available on the library's shelves, and this is not a title that Marjorie herself would have selected therefore she is compromising on her professional judgement by adding the item to stock. In addition the church group may well object to the compromise, since they see the books as being science books. The decision to compromise may well open up more problems for the school than a flat refusal would, as the church group may well see their beliefs as being demeaned by the decision.

B4.2 Misinformation highway

This response raises some large ethical issues that have to be dealt with. Jane certainly needs to discuss with the staff member exactly why supplying the information was improper. However, this may need to be handled delicately if there is to be no danger of offending the belief system of the individual. Jane should make it clear to all staff that personal belief systems have no place in the library, and certainly should never be an issue when supplying information to satisfy customer requests. Contacting the customer to 'rectify' the situation could be a major ethical challenge. The customer is already vulnerable, and to get in touch regarding such a delicate issue could greatly upset them, leading to an even larger ethical dilemma for the library service and for Jane.

B4.3 Who's promoting whom?

By carrying out the initiative in a half-hearted manner Artur is potentially selling the customers short in terms of quality of service. Regardless of whether or not he agrees with the library purchasing the materials, if he agrees to carry out the initiative he should so with all of his skill and determination. Even books purchased at a discount have cost the organisation money, and to not attempt to get maximum benefit from the purchase would be an unethical way of proceeding. In addition by not offering support to the eight community libraries he is in fact in dereliction of duty, as the staff within the eight libraries look to him for guidance on how to promote books to adult users.

B4.4 An issue of refusal to issue!

By calling on support from the senior member of staff, Grace is reinforcing the point that the item is inappropriate for the teenager. This tactic also acts as a counterpoint to any subsequent complaint the mother may make against Grace, since she has involved the senior member of staff in the decision-making process. The senior member of staff may also be more versed in library regulations and could be aware of any rules that allow staff to refuse to lend an adult item if they believe it will be placed in the hands of a minor. Ultimately, however, the DVD may well be issued to the mother after attempts at persuasion have failed and if no such statute exists in the library ordinances.

Sections C4.1 – C4.4

C4.1 Looking a gift horse in the mouth

Marjorie's approach in attempting to win the Principal round to her way of thinking is a positive response. Marjorie should be able to use the professional networks of librarians that exist, and her professional association, to advise her on pertinent points should she not have access to information and data. By placing the dilemma facing the school in a larger context and discussing how other schools have handled it, the discussion may well give the Principal the evidence and confidence to debate with any school board members who wish to question any refusal to make the material available to students. Marjorie needs to be aware that the Principal may well still refuse to adhere to her arguments and may order her to place the material on the shelves.

C4.2 Misinformation highway

Training and education should be a fundamental first port of call as a response to such a scenario occurring. It is evident that the staff member was unaware of her error, and this could have been handled simply by ensuring that in-depth training for all staff had been undertaken before they were allowed to recommend websites. In addition, ensuring the public are reminded at all times that the Internet has untrustworthy sources is a vital information literacy issue.

C4.3 Who's promoting whom?

Artur's suggested compromise of allowing staff to be involved in the selection of material from the publisher, with a new added emphasis on the promotion of creative writing and getting published, is an imaginative way of attempting to satisfy all parties. If the Library Director is adamant that the initiative go ahead, he would find it hard to refuse a request that enabled the initiative to be developed into new exciting areas, especially if it was put to him in a positive and professional way. Ultimately the publisher may object to the staff selection, but it would be in the interests of the Library Director to persuade the publisher that this compromise suits all parties and prevents any risk of controversy from the staff. Again proper evaluation of the project would allow the wisdom of the decision to be revisited at a later date, and at least the customers would have an interesting initiative that offered alternative experiences for them in addition to reading.

C4.4 An issue of refusal to issue!

Grace's refusal to issue the item to the mother may seem like the moral thing to do, but ultimately if there is no rule being broken by issuing it to her then she may find herself in trouble by making such a unilateral decision. If no rule exists in the library ordinances that backs Grace's stance then it is highly likely that she will find her decision being overruled by the senior member of staff when they are called to answer the complaint. This may well be embarrassing for Grace, but ultimately the senior member of staff may have no choice but to take the side of the mother, regardless of whether they see Grace's point or not. In the end any refusal to lend must be based on either the library rules or a decision by a responsible member of staff who can then justify the decision to the library hierarchy. Rather than refusing outright, Grace would be wiser to ask a senior member of staff to make the ultimate decision on behalf of the library service to ensure that the rules are being fairly administered.

Sections D4.1 – D4.4

D4.1 Looking a gift horse in the mouth

By refusing to place the material on the shelves Marjorie must be prepared for a potentially challenging period in her professional life. Marjorie may well find her job in jeopardy or other potential punishments are threatened for not implementing the Principal's wishes. Marjorie needs to ensure that she uses professional support networks efficiently (such as local colleagues and her professional association), and any trade union she may be a member of should also be consulted in order to ensure her position is not one she takes alone.

D4.2 Misinformation highway

Responding by reducing trust in the staff would be a detrimental step. Such a decision would suggest such a fundamental lack of faith in the wider staff that it would be severely damaging to the supervisor–staff relationship and could potentially lead to a loss in morale that impacted on service quality. Such a system would also be unworkable, and would lead to long delays in customers being assisted while staff members sought a senior member of staff to undertake duties they themselves would be easily able to fulfil given appropriate training and guidance.

D4.3 Who's promoting whom?

Artur's refusal to carry out the instruction of the Library Director has the possibility of posing extensive problems for Artur. He may feel that the Library Director has abused their position by suggesting an initiative that directly benefits a friend, but for him to accuse the Director of impropriety would be potentially libellous. Artur's suggestion that any conflicts of interest when developing programmes be considered closely is an appropriate one, but to suggest it when both sides in the argument are defending their positions has the potential of exacerbating the situation. More worryingly for Artur the refusal to undertake a direct instruction could potentially see him being liable to disciplinary action. Artur's concern with the processes involved in deciding on initiatives such as this is a perfectly acceptable one, but it may be something he has to revisit outside the heat of this particular issue.

D4.4 An issue of refusal to issue!

Despite Grace's strong feelings on the ethics of the matter, and the understandable reluctance she has to lose face in the issue, to mislead the customer is highly unethical. In addition Grace may well find herself caught in the lie when the senior member of staff is called upon to answer the complaint. When the senior member of staff finds that Grace has misled the mother, it may be the case that Grace will find herself the subject of disciplinary action for her behaviour. Ultimately Grace needs to be aware that she cannot make unilateral decisions that may lead to the organisation finding itself subject to a complaint, regardless of how correct she thinks she is.

5

Intellectual property questions

'I want to know how to copy tracks from
this CD onto my MP3 player'

The safeguarding of intellectual property has been a historic concern of librarians. While the notion of fair and equitable access to information has been uppermost in the concerns of librarians, as will be discussed in more detail in Chapter 6, it is fair to say that the belief was always that such access was with due concern for the laws related to intellectual property and copyright. Indeed, without some protection for the intellectual and creative works of authors, musicians, playwrights and other contributors to the knowledge of the world, there would be very little to store in libraries. There would also be little incentive for many authors and publishers to produce books if there was no financial reward for their work or no guarantee that their work would be properly attributed. As previously discussed, information is an asset that has a particular value: for many publishers and authors that value is inherently monetary, since they are financially rewarded for sales. More sales, in theory, leads to more book production, and the cycle of information supply continues onwards. For academic scholars and researchers, the value lies more in establishing or maintaining their reputation in their chosen field.

However, technology is increasingly proving a challenge to intellectual property rights. In the twenty-first century it is easy to digitise text, image, audio or video. It can also be done increasingly inexpensively and with limited skills. This increased challenge has led to a potentially dangerous demarcation between those advocating an increasingly stringent set of intellectual property laws, and those who advocate a freer regime where fair dealing becomes the norm.

This chapter will discuss some of the major intellectual property issues facing librarians in the twenty-first century, and present some library-based case studies dealing with those issues.

What is intellectual property?

An intellectual property right, or IPR, is a term that covers a multitude of resources. At its root the term recognises that a human being has rights over the creative works he or she produces, be it fiction, fact book, a piece of artwork or an invention. The rights spoken of do not merely relate to a right to financial compensation for sale of the item produced, although this is a fundamental part of IPR; the rights also extend to protection over use and abuse of the work. This is an important point, since it would be a breach of IPR if someone were to pay for use of a creative work and then attempt to pass it off as their own. So essentially IPR means that it is not merely the act of financially rewarding the creator, it is also the right to expect that creative work not be abused or further developed without the express agreement of the rights holder.

In an attempt to create a balance between the rights of the creator of a work and those of society to have access to the work, *fair dealing agreements* have been developed which allow a limited amount of copying and use without the need to seek agreement, e.g. the use of quotations, with acknowledgement, in works such as this or copying one article from a journal for private study or research. In Britain, these amounts are controlled through the Copyright Licensing Agency (CLA), which is considered in more detail below. However, we also consider the concern that fair dealing agreements are now under threat as rights holders seek to counter the threat from digital technologies.

This leads us to the issue of copyright, a subset of IPR. Copyright is the legal protection afforded a creative work, and can be broken down into moral rights and economic rights. Moral rights, as discussed above, are the protection offered to an author in the event that another person does attempt to pass that author's work off as their own. It also offers protection against anyone altering a creative work (adaptation). Economic rights are what people more commonly consider being copyright. The economic rights to a creative work may not necessarily lie with an author; for the most part they lie with the distributor of the creative work, normally a publisher. This system allows a business to look after the dissemination of a work and keep strict controls over who uses it, when they use it and for which purposes. It is important to note that while economic rights for a creative work are often passed on by the author, to a publisher for instance, the moral rights cannot be passed on and remain with the author or creator of the work.

It is not unreasonable for the creators and distributors of creative works to seek to protect their intellectual property. However, as Feather states, 'the difficulties arise when this legitimate desire to protect property comes into conflict with the equally legitimate needs of potential beneficiaries' (Feather, 2004: 146). Going back to two of our key ethical questions discussed in Chapter 1:

- How much control should the creator of information have over that information?

- Does an individual have the right to access any piece of information he or she needs?

Within these two questions, we can ask what is the role of the librarian, and what is his or her ethical duty and priority? Is it protection of the right of access, protection of IPR, or a balancing act between both? While the laws protecting IPR will vary from country to country, and you should certainly ensure you are aware of the laws in your own jurisdiction, the fundamental issues regarding IPR are universal and are a constant concern for librarians.

IPR and libraries

Libraries and IPR coexist on two fronts. Firstly, libraries as organisations must ensure that they themselves do not breach copyright laws. In the UK higher education sector, institutions have been required to work with a copyright collections agency that works on behalf of publishers and authors, namely the Copyright Licensing Agency or CLA. In the late 1990s the CLA focused on the predilection of universities to put together course packs for students consisting of selections of reading materials from journals and the like. The CLA felt this was a clear breach of copyright, as the material created in the course packs was tantamount to a textbook. Universities had already been paying a blanket licence that covered photocopying of materials, but the CLA felt that course packs merited a second payment. As Mendis has discussed, the 'CLA's main point was that the blanket licence fee that was being paid at the time did not cover the production of course packs and pointed out that the Licence required that Course Packs should be the subject of a separate payment and individual clearance' (Mendis, 2005: 5). This separate clearance added an extra layer of bureaucracy and expense to the process of creating course materials for students, in addition to any extra payments. Understandably universities felt this was too expensive an option for them and felt so strongly about it as a collective that they took the case to court. The judge in the case found that to clear course packs separately would add an unnecessary extra tier of bureaucracy and his findings reinforced a single blanket licence scheme.

Secondly, libraries must attempt to ensure that their users do not breach copyright. This tends to be more problematic, since in many instances the librarian may be unaware that a user may be breaching copyright on the library premises. In addition, once a library resource has been borrowed, the librarian loses any control over what is then done with it. Publishers tend to be more interested in instances where a library has *knowingly* allowed copyright to be breached – for instance, allowing a user to make multiple copies of an item. Such breaches could lead to a library being held liable for the abuse. An infamous test case from the early 1970s was centred on the publishers' concern with the then new technology of photocopiers. The University of New South Wales was sued for allowing a user to make two photocopies of a chapter of short stories, even though the library was unaware the user had carried out the photocopying. The courts found that the university was suspicious that photocopying of copyright material was occurring and thus should have done more to inform patrons of its illegality. One of the judges labelled the stance of the university library as an 'invitation to copy' (Mendis, 2005: 10). The subsequent furore surrounding the case led libraries across the globe to consider placing clear copyright notices beside photocopiers in a bid to educate users as to the potential legal liabilities.

Traditional roles versus modern challenges

Librarians continue to be concerned to ensure that, while providing access to materials, it is done within the law. Understanding of copyright has always been a fundamental requirement for librarians, since part of their remit has been to ensure the public were informed about IPR and did not abuse it on library premises.

Possibly the greatest challenge to IPR and to the librarian's ability to manage it within libraries is the development of technology. It is now relatively simple to copy practically anything, be it a document, piece of music, image or film. Given the movement of libraries to deliver more services electronically, the quality and quantity of information and communication technology (ICT) within libraries has grown, and continues to do so. It is quite common nowadays to find document scanners in even the smallest library, equipment that means intellectual property can be abused.

This historical role has not altered, but something that is changing is the attitude of wider society towards IPR, and this has a knock-on effect for new entrants to the profession. As Jones notes:

> Downloads appear to be carried out by a variety of people, including those who are otherwise law-abiding in many or all other aspects of their lives. Fisher reported that, about 5 years ago, when he asked his lecture audience in Rio de Janeiro consisting of approximately 350 Brazilian lawyers, 150 judges, and 200 law students how many of them had used Napster, around 'half raised their hands'. Although much has changed in the past 5 years, a pattern of fairly extensive non-compliance with copyright law protections of music and film files still appears to exist. (Jones, 2005: 288)

The issue is that many people see downloading as an 'OK' thing to do, and for the librarian this makes acting as an intermediary difficult. Indeed, the librarian may be someone who privately downloads at home and has to take on a different public stance.

Exacerbating the situation from the point of view of rights holders is the exponential growth in the use of file-sharing technologies, specifically peer-to-peer technologies (P2P) which allow users across the world to share files. From the point of view of liability for libraries, a case in Europe shows the potential. Conradi highlights the 2003 decision against easyinternetcafe which was deemed to be in breach of copyright law by allowing users to download music and burn the files onto CDs while on their premises and using their computer terminals for the purpose (Conradi, 2003: 289). After a protracted legal dispute, easyinternetcafe settled the case by paying the British Phonographic Industry £80,000 pounds plus their legal fees of £130,000. This case highlights the potential dangers in not being aware of what users are doing when burning material onto CDs using library computers. Unless you are 100 per cent sure about your security, it can be difficult to know if a user is doing what eventually cost easyinternetcafe £210,000 pounds.

Such a state of affairs is of obvious concern to rights holders, and their disquiet should also concern librarians. Yet it is how such matters are being addressed by rights holders that poses major ethical challenges for librarians. There is no doubt that rights holders have been winning the legislative battles when it comes to convincing law-makers that technology is having an enormous impact on their business. As Fernandez-Molina suggests:

> The copyright holders (especially the music and media industries) have run an effective campaign to convince the world (and lawmakers in particular) that their situation was getting much worse under the digital environment. This, together with pressure applied in the right places, has led to legislation breaking the traditional balance of copyright, now in favour of rightsholders. (Fernandez-Molina, 2003: 41)

A movement away from the traditional fair dealing approach forces ethical dilemmas onto librarians who have to defend what they may see as an unfair system. Indeed as Joint states, 'There are those in education and research who appear to look on certain IP matters in terms of bureaucratic constraints which should be challenged rather than obeyed' (Joint, 2006: 331).

Balancing rights with responsibilities – electronic dimensions

While technology acts as a democratic mediator by freeing up access to information, it can also be used to limit access to information. Internet filtering will be discussed in Chapter 6, but from the point of view of IPR, the main technological barrier to access lies in the realm of digital rights management or DRM. DRM software is increasingly being adopted by rights holders to provide access to intellectual property. The most popular incarnation of DRM software is probably Apple's iTunes system which is a crucial component of iPods, while another example is Windows Media Player which also has an inbuilt DRM component to control access. These systems can seek to protect IPR by making the purchase, access and delivery of a work possible only via the specific software itself. If we consider for a moment how music has been historically delivered, vinyl records were formats that could be played on any machine equipped for the purpose – you were not restricted to one specific brand of machine to play them. Similarly compact discs (CDs) were a non-proprietary delivery mechanism; all that was necessary to play them was a compact disc player of any brand. The movement to DRM for music and media delivery forces the user to stick to one proprietary format.

DRM software can also be used to deliver electronic books (eBooks), and there are examples of public libraries that have used DRM systems to do just this in the USA (Overdrive, 2003). eBooks remain at an early stage in terms of their development in libraries; however, should they become a main staple of library provision then it is highly likely we will see increasing roles for DRM software to manage their delivery to users.

Licensing of information sources and software

Another challenge for librarians in managing IPR is in the licences attached to CD- and DVD-ROM materials and web-based subscription services. For any library that purchases CD- or DVD-ROMs it is essential that they understand the range of licences that comes with the titles they buy. Some publishers allow blanket site licences that allow one title to be installed on all computers; others limit installation to one computer, or allow installations on all computers but only one simultaneous user. It can become very easy in such a landscape for a breach of licence to occur, especially if not all staff members are familiar with the requirements of each title or publisher. Obviously the move to Internet-based provision of information services means that access to the resource can be managed at the vendor end, removing the requirement for the librarian to do so. However, there remain a lot of information resources that continue to be published on either CD or DVD, especially in the area of educational software, so being aware of the risks in this area is important.

Another major concern of librarians should be software licences for applications that may be necessary to run on library computers. In larger organisations where an ICT support department is available, there may be no need for the librarian to consider the issue of applications software licences at all, as this will normally be the responsibility of that department However, in small libraries, the librarian may well be the person responsible for ensuring that the library computers are compliant.

The website of the School of Library and Information Science (SLIS) at the University of North Texas hosts a small database of copyright breaches in libraries. One of their records cites the case of a school library district in California which was found to have unlicensed copies of software running on its computers. The financial cost to the school district is cited as being over $5 million dollars (SLIS, 2001).

Plagiarism and academic dishonesty

One aspect of intellectual property theft that librarians are increasingly attempting to tackle is plagiarism or academic dishonesty. Again with improvements in technology, it is easy to find information on the Internet on almost any topic which can then be downloaded, copied and pasted into another document. It is fair to say that plagiarism is easier now than it has ever been, and librarians have a key ethical role in communicating to library users that such a practice is immoral. With technology being the ultimate cause of the rise in plagiarism, it is also the potential saviour, as plagiarism detection software is increasingly being adopted by educational establishments in attempts to uncover any instances. These continue to be imperfect solutions, however, and the main emphasis needs to be on user education, something school and college librarians are perfectly placed to do. Lampert argues that:

> Even if librarians are not assigning the essays or research projects, we are supporting the research process involved in their creation and therefore we should either provide this information to students and faculty through lecture, lecture materials or supplemental web-based handouts. Providing resources to foster a clearer understanding of what constitutes plagiarism in different disciplines increases the likelihood of greater student understanding of what measures must be taken to both cite and integrate newly found information into the research process. (Lampert, 2004: 354)

There is an inescapable logic here: since librarians are the professionals charged with communicating effective and ethical use of information resources, education on plagiarism is a natural extension of this responsibility. Joint reinforces the need to see plagiarism as a subset of IPR theft:

IP issues overlap very significantly with another area of concern in education today, plagiarism issues. After all, plagiarism occurs when one person's intellectual property is passed off as another's, with or without the agreement of the original rights owner. All academic staff deplore plagiarism and plagiarism among academic staff is a career-shortening infringement. Above all, plagiarism among students, apart from being ethically and legally unsound, deprives the plagiarising student of the benefits of true personal educational development. (Joint, 2006: 334)

Thus our role as educators becomes crucial when imparting to students the potential dangers of plagiarism.

Conclusion

Historic concerns for librarians have now become modern-day dilemmas. The reaction of rights holders to the protection of their IPR has placed enormous pressures on librarians who wish to provide access to these resources. While maintaining the traditional *photocopier watch* to ensure that users do not abuse copyright in this traditional way, the attention of librarians is increasingly moving to technological mechanisms for breaching IPR. Librarians are being forced to deliver services in an increasingly restrictive world, where IPR is delivered via DRM systems and where the library is charged with ensuring only legitimate users gain access. Legislators around the world have backed rights holders in their moves to introduce ever more stringent laws to protect their IPR, and librarians find themselves on the front line policing policies with which they may not necessarily agree. As technology improves, so will the ability to breach IPR, and with these trends we are seeing the role of librarians increasingly becoming that of an IPR police for rights holders. This runs the risk of changing the definition of librarian as 'gatekeeper' to librarian as 'sentry'. This difference in definition is not a subtle one and it is not a role that librarians have historically sought.

The case studies that follow will discuss some of the ethical dilemmas faced by librarians in the area of IPR.

Case studies

Case study 5.1 Licence revoked?

Stephanie Sutton is the librarian in a school in an inner-city area. Arriving back from a three-month absence due to illness, she finds that her assistant, Alison, has undertaken a few initiatives while she was away, including organising sessions involving use of the historically underused CD- and DVD-ROM material in the library.

Alison tells Stephanie that some of the CD-ROMs had been proving more popular than others, so in order to ensure as many students could access the popular titles as possible she had made ten copies of each of the discs for those CD-ROMs that could not be installed on the computer hard drives. For those that could be installed on the hard drives, Alison had pre-installed all workable titles so that each machine could use them simultaneously.

Stephanie is very concerned with this news, since she knows that the reason the library only had one of each title was due to the expense, and that making copies and installing titles on all computers was a major breach of the software licences. When Stephanie explains all of this to Alison, she apologises and says that the Principal knew about it and had given her permission to make the copies after she told him how popular the initiatives had been.

Stephanie meets the Principal to discuss the situation and explain her concerns and the nature of the licences for the titles concerned. The Principal tells her that no one will ever find out and that the students are benefiting from the extra access, and thus she should continue Alison's programme and leave the illegal copies on the computers until such a time as an audit of the computers may be undertaken by the local school board.

Which of the following options should Stephanie take?

A Stephanie feels that by raising the issue with the Principal she has undertaken the proper professional route, and that any breach of the licence is ultimately the Principal's decision and responsibility. She returns to the library and leaves the software installed on the computers, and allows the pupils to use the copies at future initiatives.
  Go to section A5.1

B Stephanie leaves the Principal's office determined to do some research as to how big a mistake breaching the licence could be. She contacts professional sources to find out if any schools or other libraries had ever been found in breach of software licences and if so what the liability was for the librarian and the organisation concerned. She returns to the Principal with the evidence to attempt to convince him to change his mind.

Go to section B5.1

C Stephanie refuses to carry out the Principal's instructions and instead tells him that when she returns to the library she will destroy all copies of the CD-ROMs and uninstall all copies of the other software from all but one computer.

Go to section C5.1

D Stephanie contacts a local school board member to voice her concerns and let him know about the potential liability the board is facing by the Principal's unwise decision.

Go to section D5.1

Case study 5.2 The customer is always right?

Michael Maloney is the assistant librarian in the Business Information Department of a university library. The Business Information Department occupies the third floor of the five-floor library. One morning Michael is helping a lady with an enquiry on market research information relating to children's clothing. He locates for her a market research report that due to its licence can only be read in the library and cannot be photocopied. Michael explains this to the lady, but she insists that she must have copies as she needs them for background information to a business proposal she is presenting to her bank after graduating from university later that year. Michael insists that due to the great expense of the reports, the publishers only allow libraries to store them under the strict proviso they not be copied, but the lady continues to insist she needs to photocopy the report. She suggests to him that if he turned a blind eye she could copy it and only she and he would know. Michael stresses that he cannot allow this. After unsuccessfully attempting to persuade Michael, she eventually takes the report to a desk and begins to read it. Michael returns to the counter to serve the next customer.

After ten minutes Michael notices that the lady is no longer in the room and after checking he can find no trace of the report in the department. Looking over the balcony to the floor below him he sees the lady standing in a queue waiting for the photocopier. He is unsure, but he thinks that she is holding the market research report. Michael suspects that the lady had waited until he was busy serving another user and then deliberately left the department to photocopy the document. There was no need for the lady to go anywhere else for a photocopier as the one in the department was in good working order and was currently available to use.

How should Michael handle the situation?

A Michael makes his way to the floor below to challenge the lady regarding her intention to photocopy the document after repeatedly being told by him that she was not able to do so. He takes the item from her and asks her to leave the library.
   Go to section A5.2

B Michael telephones a staff member on the floor below to ask them to politely intervene to prevent her photocopying the document. He asks them to tell the lady to return the report to the Business Information Department immediately.
   Go to section B5.2

C Michael telephones security and asks them to take the item from the lady and physically remove her from the library.
   Go to section C5.2

D Michael feels that he has done his best to protect the intellectual property of the document and that if the lady wants to go to the bother she has had to in order to photocopy it then who is he to intervene. He allows the photocopying to take place.
   Go to section D5.2

Case study 5.3 Suspicion?

Alison DiNozzo is an assistant librarian in a small public library service. During the summer she occasionally finds her duties involve covering for staff that are on vacation across the library network, thus she can find herself working in a different library each day.

One day she is allocated to work in a small community library. During the lunch break the library is staffed only by her and a library assistant, and this particular day finds the library extremely busy with users. A young woman comes to the counter with two children, who are obviously bored and are making a great deal of noise. The woman holds up a handful of CDs and asks Alison if she can make copies of her holiday photographs which have just been supplied to her on CD by the local photograph processing shop.

Alison escorts the young woman over to the nearest available computer with CD copying facilities. After quickly showing her how to use the program that copies CDs, she is about to return to the counter to serve other customers who are waiting. As she turns around she notices that in the pile of CDs is what looks like copyrighted music discs.

How should Alison handle the situation?

A As the library is extremely busy, Alison decides that to get into any kind of confrontation over the situation would be counter-productive. Since she cannot possibly know if the woman is going to copy the music CDs she feels there is no breach of copyright for her to address. She returns to the counter to serve the next customer.
   Go to section A5.3

B Alison takes the opportunity to remind the woman that by using a library computer she is automatically agreeing to the library's policy relating to copying of materials, and that she should ensure that any CDs she copies are non-copyrighted.
   Go to section B5.3

C Alison asks politely to see what the woman is copying. The woman replies that she is copying holiday photographs and they are her property, so she should be allowed to copy them without interference. Alison then asks the woman if she intends to copy the music CDs that are in the pile, to which the woman replies no, as she had just collected them from a friend and has no intention of copying them.
   Go to section C5.3

D Alison refuses to allow the woman to use the computer in light of the fact she has music CDs and Alison believes she is going to copy them. The lady becomes extremely angry and a confrontation ensues between her and Alison.
   Go to section D5.3

Case study 5.4 'Library to Go'

Caitlin Todd is the Library Director for a large metropolitan public library service. After experiencing severe pressures on her book budget,

Caitlin decides to cease purchasing printed reference works and move her entire library network's reference materials to an online service.

The project she has chosen is called 'Library to Go' and encompasses encyclopaedias, dictionaries and other fact books. Access is delivered by logging in via the user's library card number, and one of the main reasons Caitlin really liked the product was that users could use the service remotely from their own home or workplace by using their log-in. She felt this moved the library service into people's homes and workplace and was a value-added aspect to the service. Since the choice to go with this service was made due to budgetary pressures she feels that the library can be happy that while traditional sources have been lost, they have actually been replaced by something better.

Nine months into the service running, Caitlin receives a visit from the 'Library to Go' regional representative, Abby, who had marketed the system to her before she purchased it. Abby informs Caitlin that the company is concerned that the amount of access being made of the system does not represent what Caitlin paid for it. Abby relates that the company is especially concerned that one private company in the area seems to be using the service several times a day to find out information that they are obviously using for commercial purposes. Abby informs Caitlin that such use breaches the licence. Caitlin is surprised to find this, but says that she is happy that local companies are using library services. Abby tells Caitlin that given this type of usage the annual cost for the system would have to rise by 30 per cent for the next year, and that it is then up to Caitlin whether she wishes to recoup some of those costs from heavy users. Abby suggests that if the price is to remain constant then Caitlin cannot allow companies to use the service. Any such usage would be monitored and billed appropriately. Another option Abby offers is to restrict access just to public library buildings, which would mean the cost remaining affordable for Caitlin.

How should Caitlin handle this situation?

A Caitlin tells Abby she is being unreasonable and they should be happy the product was being successfully utilised. She suggests Abby return to the company and let them know their attitude risks the library service thinking twice about taking their product for a longer period. Abby replies that since 'Library to Go' is a database of various reference products their hands are tied as they have a duty to the rights holders to ensure that commercial usage of the system is billed accordingly.

Go to section A5.4

B Caitlin asks Abby to supply a list of library card numbers that they believe are using the system in this way and she will arrange for them to have their access cancelled and a letter written to them to remind them that in future they cannot use the service for commercial purposes.

   Go to section B5.4

C Caitlin suggests to Abby that the only way to keep in control of costs and to risk any future breaches of the licence is for access to be restricted to the public library facilities themselves.

   Go to section C5.4

D Caitlin asks Abby to keep access as it is and for her in the future to supply addresses of any companies who seem to be using the service for commercial purposes. She informs Abby that the library service will begin to bill any companies who breach the licence after giving them one written warning that they are in breach.

   Go to section D5.4

Case study discussions

Sections A5.1 - A5.4

A5.1 Licence revoked?

Stephanie could certainly argue that by pointing out to the Principal the breaches that were going on she had at least undertaken to pass on her concerns. However, returning to work in the library and allowing the licence breaches to continue puts her in a delicate position. Ultimately with her knowledge, the law is being broken, and this makes her responsible. Stephanie has a responsibility to the rights holders of the material she has purchased, and at the same time a responsibility to protect the organisation against potential liabilities.

A5.2 The customer is always right?

Michael is well within his rights to confront the woman and ask her to return the item to him, since she is in breach of the terms of use of the item. Asking her to leave is perhaps a step too far, but ultimately could be seen to be justified in the context of the situation. It is important in such a scenario to keep one's temper and by asking the woman to leave he has perhaps let his anger at the woman's actions get the better of him.

A5.3 Suspicion?

Allison has suspicions that the woman is going to copy the CDs, but that is all they are. With the library being busy, it is understandable that she feels her priority is to serve the customers who are waiting, but a wise option might have been for Alison to remind the woman about the rules regarding copyright without mentioning her specific concerns. There is always the opportunity for Allison to check on the woman later on if she feels that she needs to, as the copying of the CDs is unlikely to be undertaken quickly.

A5.4 'Library to Go'

This is a classic case where Caitlin should have read the small print of the licence in minute detail before she purchased. The fact that 'Library to Go' have a network of rights holders to keep happy suggests that this is no mere sales pitch by Abby to obtain a higher subscription fee from Caitlin, and that legitimate questions are being asked by rights holders over the type of usage being seen. Despite the success of the product with library users, it is unlikely that the company will be convinced that they should ignore abnormal use.

Sections B5.1 – B5.4

B5.1 Licence revoked?

By investigating just what the potential dangers for the school are, Stephanie is using her professional knowledge in a proactive way to convince the Principal that his decision is not only wrong, but that it places the school in danger of legal liability. Despite what seems like pig-headedness on the part of the Principal, Stephanie has professional knowledge that he does not have, thus arguments based on evidence and previous examples of schools being found liable may well be enough for him to see sense in this case.

B5.2 The customer is always right?

Asking a colleague on the floor where the lady is photocopying may seem like a way to avoid confrontation, but conversely asking someone else to deal with a situation he has so far managed could also be seen to be passing the buck. The colleague has not dealt with the lady and may see the same conversations being undertaken where the lady attempts to argue her case for being allowed to photocopy the document. There is also no guarantee, unless she is escorted, that she will return to the Department with the item.

B5.3 Suspicion?

This is an interesting tactic, and a sensible approach to the dilemma. Alison has no proof that the woman is going to copy the music CDs, but by reminding her of the library rules regarding copyright materials she is attempting to educate the woman, who may actually be unaware of this rule. By so doing she is also preparing the situation for the eventuality that the woman is going to copy the music CDs. Because she has issued a reminder to the woman, if she does copy the CDs Alison will be within her rights to implement the library rules, which may see the woman being asked to cease, have her access to computers limited or asked to leave the library.

B5.4 'Library to Go'

Making the library users who are using the service for commercial purposes aware of their obligations to ensure that they are using the product within the rules of the licence seems a sensible response. They may well have been oblivious to the fact that what they were doing was in any way wrong. This then means that once Caitlin has written to them she can monitor their usage and cancel access for the cards if they continue to abuse the service. It also gives her the opportunity of marketing a commercial rate access to them, and thus potentially provides a new service for the business community.

Sections C5.1 – C5.4

C5.1 Licence revoked?

Stephanie is well within her rights, as the person responsible for the library, to destroy the illegal copies of the CD-ROMs and uninstall illegal copies. The Principal may well attempt to instruct her not to do so, but he would have no basis to enforce such a command as if it went to a higher body for a decision they would no doubt come down on Stephanie's side. Certainly the Principal would be unwise to attempt to argue for the illegal copies to be maintained as liability would be seen by the board, and his competence may well come into question. Ultimately, however, Stephanie may find by making this decision that she has burnt bridges with the Principal for the future.

C5.2 The customer is always right?

Involving security and making a drama out of a crisis could be seen as an overreaction to the incident. Although it may have the desired effect on the lady and communicate that the library is serious about enforcing copyright licences, it may also lead to an escalated incident if she reacts angrily to security escorting her from the premises. It also passes the resolution of the incident from the person who is aware of all of the issues, i.e. Michael, to staff members who are oblivious to it.

C5.3 Suspicion?

By directly asking the question about the woman's intentions, Alison is getting to the root of her suspicions. This also means that she can at the same time reinforce to the woman the rules regarding copying of copyright materials in the library. Such an approach perhaps runs the risk of the woman feeling aggrieved at being suspected of breaching the rules, but if done so in a polite manner the chances are it will not. Ultimately the success of this approach will depend on the politeness and approachability of Alison and her skills in being able to not come across as being accusatory or suspicious. By asking the question and reinforcing the library rules, Alison is also able to react if she does later find the woman copying the music CDs.

C5.4 'Library to Go'

Having access restricted to just library buildings is one way of ensuring tighter control over usage; however, it means a value-added aspect to the service is being removed. There is a good chance that a lot of goodwill with users will be lost from those who have found home access to be useful to them. While this decision may address the problem at hand, it will impact on all other users, and as such is a questionable decision from the point of view of service quality.

Sections D5.1 – D5.4

D5.1 Licence revoked?

Stephanie may well feel she is within her rights to go above the Principal's head, but this should really be a position of last resort. Unless she feels convinced that she has tried everything she can to persuade the Principal his decision is wrong, to undermine him in this way may lead to problems for her in the future.

D5.2 The customer is always right?

Michael may well feel it is not worth the effort to pursue the lady's breach of copyright, but in that case why spend so much time stating the position of the library in the first place? While he may agree that the copyright rules for the document are excessive, he has a duty to ensure that if he is aware of any photocopying of the item he seeks to stop it. There is a minute chance the lady may even be someone testing the copyright regime within the library, but even if this is the case, consistency of approach and adopting the correct legal response on each occasion is important. It is not really an ethical option for Michael to ignore the woman breaking the law.

D5.3 Suspicion?

This is a particularly problematic response to the situation by Alison. She has no proof that the woman intends to copy the music CDs, and she has essentially accused the woman of breaking rules before she has done so, and worse, that she intends to break the law. If the woman had no such intentions, Alison has very possibly offended her in a busy public building. The ensuing confrontation now has to be managed appropriately, and given how busy the library is it is a situation that could likely impact on service for other library users and her colleague who will now have to take on serving all of the customers while Alison attempts to resolve the situation.

D5.4 'Library to Go'

Deciding to bill the companies who have been found to be abusing the licence would be one way of recouping the costs; however, it is quite possible that the companies may be unaware that an employee is using the service for their own purposes. Legally the library would have no way of enforcing the requests for payment for these services, since the library had made no agreement with the company concerned. A more sensible approach would be for Caitlin to send the company concerned a warning letter regarding the abnormal usage and offer a commercial service to them that could be billed at corporate rates.

6

Freedom of access, privacy and acceptable use

'What did that suspicious-looking man in scruffy clothes borrow last week?'

This chapter will deal with some fundamental issues, but issues that are currently hotly debated both within society and within librarianship generally. Historically libraries have partly served to remove the disparity between the information haves and have-nots. Part of this was the belief that equity of access was a vital democratic function. Coupled with this was the belief that the right to user privacy should also be cherished. Indeed, contemporaneously, both equity of access and privacy stand tall as two of Gorman's enduring values (Gorman, 2000).

Yet managing access for users in the digital world poses great challenges. Use that is deemed inappropriate becomes an issue between those who believe users should have access to all knowledge, and those who equally believe that there are some types of information libraries should not provide, such as pornography, e-mail, games and chat rooms. Like many ethical issues discussed in this book, both sides of the debate have legitimacy to their arguments, but this makes decisions all the more challenging in the front line of service provision.

The focus of this chapter will be a discussion of four of the key ethical questions identified in the first chapter, namely:

- How much control should an individual have over the information that pertains to them?

- Does an individual have the right to access any piece of information he or she needs?

- Is there a duty to make certain information inaccessible when appropriate?
- Is there a duty to make information fully accessible and findable?

As with previous chapters, case studies will be presented after the discussion to highlight some of the practical challenges faced by librarians and the range of ethical choices available to them.

Equity of access

Equity of access to knowledge and information has been and continues to be a key concern for the library profession; indeed, as we saw in the discussion of ethical codes, many of the professional associations representing librarians place equity of access as a core mission. Gorman defines equity of access in the following way:

> Equity of access ... means that everyone deserves and should be given the recorded knowledge and information she wants, no matter who she is and no matter in what format that knowledge and information is contained. It means that one should be able to have access (either to a library building or from a remote location), that library services should assist in the optimal use of library resources, and that those resources should be relevant and worthwhile. (Gorman, 2000: 133)

This very much mirrors the beliefs of key library thinkers such as Ranganathan as well as professional associations. For instance, in the UK, CILIP's Ethical Code of Practice states that librarians should show, 'commitment to the defence, and the advancement, of access to information, ideas and works of the imagination' (CILIP, 2006c). The Australian Library and Information Association (ALIA) mirrors this by stating that part of the mission of its members is:

> Promotion of the free flow of information and ideas through open access to recorded knowledge, information, and creative works. *We assert that this access across time and across cultures is fundamental to a thriving culture, economy and democracy.* (ALIA, 2002; emphasis in original)

Internationally IFLA's Free Access to Information and Freedom of Expression (FAIFE) Committee deals with issues relating to equity of access on behalf of the world's librarians. It argues that:

> The right to know and the freedom to express are two aspects of the same principle. The freedom of expression is realized by the preservation of the right to know. The right to know is related inherently to the freedom of thought and conscience and all other fundamental human rights. Freedom of thought and freedom of expression are necessary conditions for the freedom of access to information. (IFLA, 2005)

Equity of access, then, continues to be a key concern for librarians worldwide.

Yet it would be churlish to ignore the fact that a belief in the equity of access does not necessarily equate to equal access for all. As a mission for librarians to achieve it should remain, but in reality even in the developed world complete equity of access is a myth. Take, for example, the services available to the university student versus those available to the public library customer. Part of a university's remit is to make available works of a scholarly nature, including vast runs of periodical literature and peer-reviewed publications. Invariably this material is becoming available electronically and via large database systems to which the university subscribes. Students normally access such material via campus computers or via a password supplied by the university library. Public libraries very often do not put access to scholarly periodicals at the top of their agenda, understandably given their financial priorities. Therefore for the life-long learner access to such works can be problematic and piecemeal at best. This is a straightforward example of equity of access not being achieved, and it is purely a case of simple economics. There will never be enough money for a library to grant access to the world's knowledge to their users: it is a laudable aim, but an increasingly unrealistic one.

This is even more the case in the developing world, where even universities cannot afford access to scholarly works which are essential for the development of their economies and their professions. Equity of access for such countries becomes more than a mere mission for a profession, but an essential component of that society's development into a knowledge economy. In other aspects such access also becomes a democratic necessity if the populace are to be given the information they need to question decisions made by government and bureaucrats.

Barriers to access

Notwithstanding the user's inability to access library holdings that are not there, equity of access also relates to other barriers to access, including the physical and non-physical. For instance, library buildings themselves can become barriers to access, both literally and metaphorically. Many libraries are buildings of historic importance: the unprecedented building programme of the early twentieth century constituted by the generosity of philanthropist Andrew Carnegie saw some 3,000 public libraries constructed worldwide. Many of these libraries still remain to this day, and continue to be cherished for their architecture. However, old buildings bring potential access problems and it is fair to say that many of these libraries (and many since) were not constructed with the less able-bodied user in mind. Physical disability can pose tremendous problems in accessing many library buildings, and libraries have a moral duty to ensure all citizens can access the services on offer. This is easier said than done, with many libraries posing significant problems in terms of the ability to alter their infrastructure to allow disabled users to enter. In the UK the Disability Discrimination Act 1995 puts priority of access to buildings as a key aspect of equal rights for disabled users. Libraries must make their buildings as accessible as possible within reason, and this can be an expensive undertaking. Similarly, in the USA the Americans with Disabilities Act 1990 sought to make sure people with disabilities were not disadvantaged when accessing services. It is no surprise to see many libraries start from scratch and move to new modern, accessible premises as a result of such legislation, given the inadequacy of many library buildings.

Disability also needs to be considered when delivering electronic services. With more and more services now available remotely, it is essential that libraries make their Internet presence accessible to all users. Within the library premises itself, libraries must ensure that adaptive technologies are available for users who need them; these can be anything from large-key keyboards to tracker balls that replace standard mice. This may also involve the purchase of specific software that reads pages aloud for the visually impaired. All of these issues relate to equity of access and are ethical duties for librarians, notwithstanding any overarching legal duty.

Equity of access can also relate to where a building is sited. Many public libraries may have been constructed during the Carnegie era in a location that was then the heart of the community. Communities, like libraries, are growing organisms and may spread in such a way that the library is no longer at its centre. This can often pose severe problems of access when the library is perhaps not situated on public transport routes. Even when transport is available, other factors may come into play. A situation faced by one of the authors in his time in practice was a public library that serviced a large inner-city community where a large number of children could not access their local library because it was situated in an area that was the domain of a specific children's gang. This may seem trivial, but to the children who were too frightened to visit the library due to fear of being attacked, it was a major barrier to access. This was addressed only partially, with the library service funding a weekly bus service for the children concerned that transported them from their home area to the public library and back again. This only addressed the issue on a surface level, but it was at least a commitment to the notion of equity of access. Addressing such quandaries may well be a daily task for librarians in inner-city libraries worldwide, and responding positively to them is an ethical concern. Certainly being aware of such a barrier and not attempting to address it could be argued as being unethical.

Another hugely controversial area is that of opening hours. In terms of equity of access this absolutely crucial. A closed building is as inaccessible as it gets. Yet it is common, when finances are an issue, for opening hours to be the target of cost-cutting. Often this is seen as the lesser of two evils, the other option being full closure. Yet while the pragmatism of keeping a library open under restricted hours may save a service point, it is also likely to have an impact on equity of access. Issues of materials may well go down, but even if they do not in the short term, 'over the long term reductions both in opening hours and materials spending are likely to have an impact on levels of materials issues although this may not be discernible for up to two years after a cut' (Loynes and Proctor, 2000: 622). Again, when deciding on reducing opening hours, there is more than a fiscal concern that needs to be considered. The ethics of reducing the service quality must be considered if short-term 'band aid' solutions to finance are not to become long-term barriers to equity of access.

Privacy

Privacy differs from confidentiality and security. Privacy is the overriding concept which involves the right to be left alone and the autonomy to determine with whom we share details of our personal lives or personal information. Confidentiality is a narrower concept. Violation of confidentiality undermines privacy but privacy can be achieved without confidentiality in that you can choose not to share your information in the first place and thereby not entrust others to keep it confidential. In the context of library membership it is difficult to see how individuals can gain full access to services without passing on their personal data, however. Security is necessary to maintain confidentiality and therefore privacy, as stored data need to be kept securely and be accessible only to those who need it for the purposes for which it was provided.

Privacy has also to be balanced against other values. As with other rights, there are trade-offs and competing rights and interests which need to be respected. Economic interests may cause consumers to trade privacy for convenience such as occurs in credit card shopping. Efficient government requires personal information for taxation, health care, etc. Privacy can also conflict with publicly accepted principles of law enforcement and public safety.

It could be argued that privacy is beginning to become a potentially old-fashioned concept. The increasing desire of our governments and the businesses we use to know more about us is impinging more on our day-to-day lives. Registering for many web-based services sees us having to tick boxes to unsubscribe from mailings or to ensure we do not have our data passed on to 'selected third parties'. Individuals and organisations increasingly have to spend money on spam and junk mail filters to attempt to ensure that their e-mail inbox is not stuffed with inappropriate mails offering dubious services. This is all, at the very least, an inconvenience, and at the worst offers the potential for personal information to be abused or misused.

In the context of libraries we must consider two separate but equally vital issues:

- user privacy as it relates to their successful use of library resources;
- privacy of the user's personal data.

User privacy when using library materials

It is inconceivable that a librarian would look over the shoulder of a user to see which book he or she is reading. The thought is anathema to what libraries and librarians do. The post 9/11 scenario seems to be that trust is now something we cannot afford – whether accurate or not, an extremely sad state of affairs indeed. Even before the tragedy of 9/11 there was an increasing pressure on librarians who were delivering the Internet to users. The nature of the Internet and some of the information therein led many in society to challenge what they saw as inappropriate material being made available in the public, school and university library. Measures to control this were brought in, and this included developing acceptable use policies (AUPs) that each user would have to agree to before being given Internet access. Their purpose was to define what constituted acceptable use of the library facilities. This was a useful management tool for many organisation, but at its root it is an attack on equity of access, since it defines some information as inappropriate. This is entirely understandable when the issue of child protection is the goal; no right-minded individual would wish children to be exposed to pornographic content when visiting their public or school library. However, many policies define sites such as chat rooms, gambling sites and games sites as being inappropriate. Is this a value judgement that can be made in the twenty-first century with any degree of credibility? It is oft posited that libraries should move with the times, and as people become more and more familiar with the many uses of the Internet, the bar on anything but information use within a library becomes difficult to sustain ethically.

The second measure introduced by many libraries, and perhaps the most controversial, was the software-based solution of Internet filtering. While AUPs define in a general fashion what is and is not acceptable use of the Internet, filtering software goes that step further and blocks any information it is programmed to block, either by using keywords or a list of banned addresses, or a combination of both. While it is certainly true that, as Hauptman puts it, 'unfiltered access to the Internet presents some major ethical challenges even to those whose commitment to intellectual freedom is unequivocal,' it is equally true that 'it is not our business to mediate between users and the virtual world' (Hauptman, 2002: 65) It could be argued that many organisations ventured down the filtering route to protect themselves rather than in a bid to halt intellectual freedom, but this makes the decision even more problematic for an ethical professional. The problem with filtering is that while it may block material that is offensive or questionable (though the question remains to whom), it has also been found to block material of a legitimate nature, and often this material is of personal or sensitive importance to a user, such as health information or information on sexuality. Any library professional should feel troubled if such a scenario exists in their service, as failure to provide a service is just that – a failure. The problems with filtering have been defined thus:

> First, under-blocking occurs when content is not blocked that should be restricted. Second, over-blocking occurs when content is blocked that should not have been restricted. Steps can be taken to reduce the frequency of errors, and to reduce their costs (for example, by providing easy appeals processes, quick overrides, and corrections) but some errors are inevitable. (Resnick et al., 2004: 67)

Errors are inevitable, but are they welcome? It could be argued that it is the clumsiness of filtering software that poses the largest ethical concern; it will never be 100 per cent accurate, even if it ever becomes 99.9 per cent accurate. Taking the human out of assessing information for a user is always a bad thing, but to put it in the hands of a software program is clumsy in the extreme. Combating the ignorance of many stakeholders with regard to the accuracy of filtering is also a challenge of the twenty-first century facing LIS professionals. When and if an inappropriate access occurs it can cause major controversy for the library, and an organisation that feels it is protected is one operating under a false sense of security. As Gorman succinctly puts it, 'the truth is that filtering systems *do not work* and they *never will work!*' (Gorman, 2000: 96). It is sad to see a situation in which many librarians worldwide are placing the vital job of information delivery in a system that is not fit for the job. Whether introduced willingly or unwillingly, the use of filtering technologies in libraries of any kind is a major ethical concern. Regardless of which side a librarian comes down on in the debate, it is essential that all are aware of all of the implications that using the software may bring when making a decision.

Privacy of the user's personal data

For those countries which have legislated for data protection, a core set of principles tend to govern their actions. These principles embody rights the user has with regard to the information that is stored about them, and include:

- a right to inspect the information;
- a right to have it corrected if it is erroneous;

- a right to sue for compensation if wrongful information has caused them damage;
- in some instances, a right to object to such information being held at all.

Data protection began to concern society in the late 1960s and early 1970s when the dawn of new technologies made it possible for organisations to electronically store information on individuals. The growth in the amount of information being gathered on individuals and the creation of large databases, not least by government, combined with the ability to link information across such databases have brought the issue of data protection to the attention of the public, most recently in the consultation on identity cards, itself a reaction to the growth in terrorism since 9/11. Growth in database marketing and the activities of credit reference agencies which utilise such large databases have also raised public awareness about how much personal information is held in electronic form and the negative consequences which can ensue should such information be found to be inaccurate. There is growing concern over civil liberties and personal privacy, especially in respect of personal data contained in, for example, medical, financial and employment records.

Data protection legislation varies considerably across the world in the degree of protection which it actually affords the individual. For example, in Britain the current legislation governing the processing of personal data is the Data Protection Act 1998 (which came into force in March 2000 and superseded the Data Protection Act 1984). The fundamental principles are the same as in the 1984 Act, although the main difference is that the Data Protection Act 1998 also covers the processing of manual data as well as data processed automatically. Therefore the Act covers electronic processing and handling as well as paper records. All such personal data must be collected, stored and used in accordance with a set of data protection principles and anyone who keeps such personal data must register this fact and state how the data will be used.

One of the main challenges facing librarians with regard to data protection is the communication to the user of just how important their personal data can be. The more services that transfer to the Internet, and the more users who begin to use library ICT facilities, the more opportunities exist for users to visit websites and pass on their personal data to websites that may abuse that information. Librarians should certainly communicate this in any user education they undertake about using the Internet. This is especially important if the library offers children and young people access to the Internet, since they need to be aware that passing on their personal details while online can be dangerous. Certainly it would be problematic for a librarian to assume that young users were already fully aware of the dangers of passing on their details, and there would be an obvious ethical duty to educate the young user in this area.

Privacy and the war on terror

Perhaps the most controversial issue related to privacy and libraries in recent years is the concentration of legislation aimed at combating the 'war on terror' in the aftermath of the 9/11 attacks. Libraries came to the fore in the debate for a crucial main reason: it was revealed that some of the terrorists who were involved in the attacks had used public library computers, an issue a Florida librarian raised with the police after the attacks (Hauptman, 2002: 40). In the immediate aftermath of the attacks this was a major development, since early theories had suggested that the terrorists had used web-based e-mail to communicate, and there were even stories in the media that suggested that the terrorists were passing secrets and plans to each other within coded computer images. It has also recently been revealed that two of the terrorists used public library computers in New Jersey to order the airline tickets for the 9/11 attack (Oder, 2005). Understandably such developments make the population generally, and the law-makers specifically, look at free and unfettered Internet access in public libraries as a potential liability. It also makes library staff question the bona fides of users in ways which would have been undreamt of on 10 September 2001.

Yet the main ethical challenges facing librarians relate to the legislation that has been introduced since 9/11 and its impact on the workings of the library. In the US the introduction in 2001 of the Patriot Act, or to give it its full title the Uniting and Strengthening America by Providing Appropriate Tools Required to Intercept and Obstruct Terrorism Act, introduced the ability for law enforcement agencies to serve National Security Letters, or NSLs, on organisations in a bid to gain information on potential terrorist suspects. NSLs are not only a library issue; they can be served on any organisation from libraries to companies to gymnasiums. The John Doe case discussed in Chapter 2 was as a direct result of an NSL being served on a Connecticut public library which the librarians concerned felt it was their ethical duty to challenge. Their recent victory in the case has in no way lessened the use of NSLs by law enforcement, although it did raise the issue of how far the FBI was prepared to go to gain the data they wanted.

In the UK several library partners, including CILIP, the British Library, the National Library of Scotland and other library agencies, joined forces to lobby against a provision in a proposed Act of Parliament that would have made it illegal for any organisation to supply someone with information that could be deemed to be promoting terrorism. This was obviously a clause that greatly concerned librarians, who felt that they could be accused of abetting a terrorist by the mere action of issuing a book or providing a computer. Much lobbying of the government took place and in the end the clause was removed from the Act, which was passed in March 2006 to become the Terrorist Act (CILIP, 2006d).

We need to be careful as a society that we are not sacrificing our freedoms in the war on terror. As Nijboer has stated, 'society must not fight terrorism in a way that destroys democracy. We do not want to accept terrorists' methods and maybe walk into a trap that will have given them a major victory' (Nijboer, 2002: 260).

Conclusion

In conclusion, it can be seen that the historic concerns of librarians relating to equity of access and privacy remain as vital today as they did over 100 years ago. If anything, their importance has increased. Both are key areas where librarians and their associations have fought for their voices to be heard on behalf of the user.

Certainly times are harder and the voices have to be raised louder to be heard; but despite the worries of those who feel civil liberties are being eroded without any effective advocacy, the successes of the John Doe librarians in raising their ethical dilemma with the world's news media illustrates that people continue to care about such issues and are willing to support committed professionals who wish to stand up for such rights. The success of the advocacy in the UK over the Terrorism Act 2006 is another example of how the historical ethical principles of librarians can be argued successfully if undertaken in a professional and organised way.

The case studies that follow will deal with some of the issues discussed within this chapter.

Case studies

Case study 6.1 The right to know?

Alice McNeill is the branch librarian in a rural village public library. The library serves a small, tightly knit community and thus users and staff know each other very well, with most staff members living in or near the village.

When shopping in the village store one day, Alice is approached by a local lady who confronts her by saying that she was disappointed that Alice did not stop her 14-year-old daughter from accessing information on contraception on a library Internet terminal. Alice tells the lady that she was unaware her daughter had sought such information, but that even if she had been aware that she would not have passed on that information to her mother, as the daughter had a right to privacy. This angers the mother, who leaves telling her that she is relieved that not all of the library staff are as inconsiderate as the librarian.

Alice is concerned that a member of library staff may have told the mother about the girl's visit to the library, and is extremely disappointed that any of her staff could betray user trust in that way, regardless of how closely they knew the mother. Next day in the library Alice begins to ask her staff if they knew of who had passed on the information. It becomes clear very quickly that the person who passed on the information, Janet, is a member of staff who happens to be a neighbour of the mother and the girl, and when confronted about the issue she happily confesses, suggesting that Alice is overreacting and that the mother had a right to know.

Which of the following approaches should Alice take?

A Alice decides to take Janet aside for a long chat to explain exactly why she feels so angry about what Janet did. She informs her that she wishes her to undertake a training course on data protection legislation, and if she refuses she will have no option but to instigate disciplinary action against her.
   Go to section A6.1

B Alice is so incensed by Janet's actions that she contacts the Human Resources Department immediately and requests that she be suspended pending an investigation into exactly what happened.
   Go to section B6.1

C Alice rebukes Janet and tells her in no uncertain terms that her actions were unacceptable. She informs her that she must write a letter of apology to the girl.

Go to section C6.1

D Alice ignores the actions of Janet in the hope that the incident will go no further.

Go to section D6.1

Case study 6.2 Access to all information?

Alana Boyd is an Arts subject librarian in a university library. One morning while staffing the information desk, a user explains that the filtering software being used by the library is blocking access to sites that are essential to his research. Alana enquires as to the nature of the sites, and the user explains that the sites are pornographic and the focus of his PhD study is societal impacts of pornography on the Internet. She explains that accessing pornographic material is against the library regulations and apologises. However, the user becomes insistent that as a registered research student he should be able to access all relevant materials necessary for his research.

Again, Alana apologises and explains to the user that accessing the sites may in fact be illegal depending on the content on them, and this may make the university liable if they purposely unblock the sites in order for a user to access them. The user tells her that not all of the sites contain illegal material, only material of a graphically sexual nature. Alana reiterates that despite the potential legality of the sites, they would be against the acceptable use policy of the university and as such she cannot offer access. The user becomes more frustrated and insists that the university is the only location where he can access the Internet. The incident is not resolved to his satisfaction and he informs Alana that he will be complaining to his research supervisor. The next day, the professor supervising the student contacts Alana to insist that his student is allowed to access the sites he requires, and that he shall take full responsibility for any liability incurred. He states that if she does not arrange for this to happen that he will complain to the University Librarian.

Which of the following approaches should Alana take?

A Alana reinforces to the Professor that the library cannot allow access to sites of that nature, no matter what the need is. She tells him that in

no way can he take responsibility for another person's search, and in any case, as the provider, ultimately the library would be responsible.
    Go to section A6.2

B Alana simply tells the Professor that he will have to contact the University Librarian with his concerns, as she is no longer in a position to help him.
    Go to section B6.2

C Alana offers to forego the university policy on this occasion and meet with the researcher again to see if any of the sites would be possible to look at without placing the researcher or university in a position of breaking the law.
    Go to section C6.2

D Alana relents on her earlier decision and offers to unblock the sites for the researcher on request, as long as he undertakes his search in a secluded area.
    Go to section D6.2

Case study 6.3 Panic out of a crisis?

Alex Hannah is the systems librarian with responsibility for Internet services for a public library system of 15 branch libraries. One afternoon he receives a call from the Library Director in a state of agitation who informs him that a parent has complained in a branch after finding out that her son had been viewing pornography on an Internet terminal. She discovered this via pictures he had saved to a disk while in the library for viewing on his home computer. The problem had the potential to get larger as the parent had claimed when leaving the library that she was going to report the incident to the local newspaper. The Library Director asks Alex to immediately close down Internet access for the entire library service pending the outcome of an investigation into this incident. Alex believes that the Director is overreacting but does so anyway. The Director asks Alex to produce a list of websites accessed by the specific machine at the time the parent claims the child had viewed and downloaded the image.

The following day a reporter from the local newspaper contacts the Library Director for a quote, to which the Library Director states that the Internet should have been filtered as it had been decided by senior management to do so, but that the evaluations of which system to buy had been taking longer than expected. He informs the reporter that the

Internet would be offline in the library service until a filtering system had been identified, purchased and installed. The story makes it into the next morning's newspaper which Alex and all his colleagues read.

As the person charged with evaluating the different potential systems referred to in the article Alex is angry at the Director's insinuation that the incident was somehow his fault for dragging his heels on the evaluations. In actual fact Alex had recommended a system months earlier but the senior management team had put it on the backburner because of the prohibitive costs. Thus Alex feels it is their responsibility that the child accessed the image.

The Library Director summons Alex to his office and instructs him to procure and install the system he had recommended months ago, and to have it ready to run within a week.

How should Alex handle this situation, bearing in mind his grievances?

A Alex feels so aggrieved at the insinuation of the Library Director that he contacts the journalist direct, but without the knowledge of his employer, to set the record straight. He informs the journalist that the only reason filtering had not been installed was due to the senior management team not being willing to spend the sum involved.

Go to section A6.3

B Alex makes his disappointment clear to the Library Director and asks for an apology. The Director refuses and rebukes Alex for his disrespect. He reinforces to Alex that he expects the filtering software to be installed and operational within the week. Alex informs him that his timetable is unreasonable and had he authorised installation of the system when it had been recommended this would not have happened.

Go to section B6.3

C Alex begins by informing the Director that he feels slighted, but he will leave his comments at that. He informs the Director that his timetable is unreasonable and that he needs more time to ensure the filtering is working properly. He informs the Director that if the filtering is too stringent it will block legitimate material and if too lenient it will allow material through of the type that caused the controversy.

Go to section C6.3

D Alex does not comment and merely leaves the Director's office to begin the process of procurement and installation.

Go to section D6.3

Case study 6.4 The library snoop

Sasha Alexandria is the head of a large academic library. It serves a world-famous university which has research strengths in a range of disciplines, from science and engineering through to arts and humanities. Sasha's library is correspondingly large, with a large book and journal stock, access to a range of databases and facilities to allow hundreds of students to access workstations. It is a multi-site library, split so that its various parts can serve certain faculties and departments.

One morning Sasha receives an e-mail from a member of library staff known (behind her back) as Snooping Susie. She has complained in the past to her site manager about things she says she has observed students doing on the workstations in the site's general access suite. These have ranged from allegations of viewing pornography to plagiarism. None have ever been substantiated. This time the e-mail (which has not been sent to Susie's site manager) complains that a certain overseas student, Mr X, always uses the same workstation, one at the very rear of the access suite which staff cannot see unless they leave the Enquiry desk and walk to the other end of the library. She alleges that he waits until that workstation is free and then stays on it until the library closes. Every time that she has tried to see what he is doing on it, he switches screens quickly and brings up a document that he appears to work on. She says that his behaviour appears odd to her and she thinks that something should be done. Because he only uses this one machine she wants it 'bugged' or a hidden camera rigged up to view its screen.

Which of the following decisions should Sasha take?

A Sasha forwards the e-mail to Susie's site manager and tells her to deal with it.

   Go to section A6.4

B Sasha forwards the e-mail to Susie's site manager and requests a meeting with her and Susie. Sasha is annoyed that Susie keeps trying to spy on students using workstations. Sasha wants to tell her to stop this and do something more useful instead.

   Go to section B6.4

C Sasha forwards the e-mail to the department in which Mr X is a student and asks if there is anything unusual in their experience about this student.

   Go to section C6.4

D Sasha deletes the e-mail and does not respond.
Go to section D6.4

Case study discussions

Sections A6.1 – A6.4

A6.1 The right to know?

Certainly there is a need to let Janet know how serious a breach of client confidentiality her actions were. Indeed, in many countries what she did is an illegal act which could have made the library accountable. Alice is wise to see the need for training for Janet to reinforce her knowledge of data protection, but given she undertook her actions for a friend there is no guarantee that the training will have the desired effect. Alice's desire not to involve disciplinary proceedings unless Janet refuses is admirable, but ultimately Alice may well be storing problems for herself, given the seriousness of the action. If Alice ignores the action and something similar happens in the future, she may find herself subject to serious disciplinary action for not reporting it to the appropriate senior member of staff. There is also no guarantee that the girl will not complain if she discovers how her mother found out, and thus Alice's attempts to keep the incident quiet may show loyalty to Janet more than the girl or the library service.

A6.2 Access to *all* information?

Alana is within her rights to reinforce to the professor that the library regulations cannot be breached on this matter. Ultimately the professor cannot take responsibility for the Internet searching of one of his students, and as such any breaches of the library and university policy would be the university's responsibility. Due to the nature of the material being requested, Alana could be seen to be looking after the interests of the organisation before those of the user, but in this case that may well be justified.

A6.3 A panic out of a crisis?

Alex's anger is understandable given the circumstances, but by contacting the journalist he has potentially brought his library service into further disrepute, and more seriously for himself has potentially placed his own job at risk. The story the Director told the journalist may well have been untrue, but it served to limit the life of the story and the potential embarrassment to the organisation. Alex's decision may well ensure the story continues to run in the newspaper, and given his position in the organisation it is likely he will be the first person suspected of speaking to the journalist. In this case it could be argued that he has looked after his own interests at the expense of his organisation's.

A6.4 The library snoop

This is a sensible response. Ultimately Susie has bypassed the appropriate chain of command (in all likelihood deliberately) by coming straight to Sasha and ignoring her line manager. Susie's line manager can discuss the e-mail with her, discipline her or investigate, depending on how seriously she takes the accusations. The incident may well end up back at Sasha's desk, but only once appropriate channels have been followed. It is important that Sasha reinforces the chain of command that exists and this decision helps to do that.

Sections B6.1 – B6.4

B6.1 The right to know?

Unfortunately for Janet, Alice may have no option but to report the incident to HRM and to instigate disciplinary action. Ultimately what Janet has done is a major ethical and legal breach that could have serious ramifications for the library service. Alice's duty to the user may outweigh her duty to Janet with such a serious incident. Janet is also attempting to do right by the organisation by making them aware of the incident and allowing them to address it.

B6.2 Access to *all* information?

Passing on the request to the person in the organisation who has the ultimate say may well be a sensible move, but it may also be the case that the University Librarian may see this as a straightforward case that Alana should be handling based on the regulations that are currently in force. Certainly it is the case that the professor is more likely to accept a 'no' from the final arbiter, but Alana's decision is perfectly justifiable in the context of the rules and she should be able to reinforce that decision without recourse to senior staff. Unless the user himself has asked for the case to be passed on, it could be argued that Alana is passing the buck by attempting to do so.

B6.3 A panic out of a crisis?

Alex is certainly within his rights to ask the Director for an apology given how he has behaved. However, since it has only angered the Director it puts Alex in a difficult position when it comes to explaining to the Director how unrealistic his timetable is for implementing the new filtering system. It is clear that the Director does not understand what is involved in the implementation, but it is also clear that since he is now angry with Alex he is unwilling to listen to him. It now means that in the short term at least Alex's professional judgement will be ignored once again, which may lead to potential problems for both Alex and the library service when the software is not ready in time. Perhaps Alex would have been better served by leaving aside his personal feelings and addressing the serious issue facing the organisation.

B6.4 The library snoop

This is a sensible response. Ultimately Susie has bypassed the appropriate chain of command (in all likelihood deliberately) by coming straight to Sasha. A meeting with Susie's line manager involved can have both Sasha and the line manager reinforcing to Susie that her behaviour is unacceptable. A decision point would be whether or not it is felt the actions merit disciplinary proceedings. But ultimately any meeting would only be a success if Susie's behaviour altered for the better. It would certainly have to be made clear to Susie how seriously her behaviour is taken by the senior staff, and that they expect her to alter it.

Sections C6.1 – C6.4

C6.1 The right to know?

Is this really an incident that an apology can fix? This is a serious breach of client confidentiality and Janet has abused her position of trust in a very serious way. A rebuke may well make Janet aware of her mistake, but ultimately Alice may have to instigate formal disciplinary proceedings in a bid to protect the library service from any potential ramifications. As much as Alice may feel that Janet has learned from her mistakes, ultimately the decision on how to proceed may be out of her hands. She should at least seek counsel from a senior colleague on how to ensure the proper channels are followed.

C6.2 Access to *all* information?

By making this decision Alana could be seen to be caving in to the pressure applied by the professor. She should certainly think twice about altering the regulations unless she can be absolutely sure that the sites being looked at are legal for the jurisdiction in which she operates. Even so, the Internet service provider used by the library service may have to be consulted before she can make such a decision, since as provider to the library they may well be unhappy at the regulations being waived.

C6.3 A panic out of a crisis?

By addressing his grievance as a comment at the beginning of the meeting before moving on to discuss the professional issue at hand, Alex at least still has the ear of the Director when he explains that the proposed timetable is unreasonable. The chance remains that the Director will not alter the timetable, but given he is still calm, he may well offer Alex any assistance he may need to ensure that the software can be implemented as quickly as possible. By keeping a cool head Alex can help to ensure that the potential damage to the library can be minimal and that he can receive the resources he needs to ensure the project is carried out efficiently.

C6.4 The library snoop

Firstly, this is a potential invasion of privacy, since there is nothing intrinsically wrong with a student using the same machine nor trying to hide what they are doing. Second, by spreading a rumour about the student, Sasha is potentially making life more difficult for an overseas student. There is no evidence that the student has done anything, and thus to escalate the incident by involving another department would be inappropriate at this stage. The student has a right to privacy, and it is highly unlikely that the other department would consider sharing gossip with the library anyway, so such a request is likely to be futile.

Sections D6.1 – D6.4

D6.1 The right to know?

Ignoring the incident is not a sensible option for Alice to pursue. The seriousness of the incident suggests that Alice will need to pass the matter to a senior colleague for a decision, and she should certainly seek senior colleagues' opinions on what to do. Ultimately the library service may be liable for the data protection breach, and this means the decision should not be made by her alone.

D6.2 Access to *all* information?

Alana is clearly bowing to the pressures placed on her by the professor. By unblocking the sites herself she is ultimately taking full responsibility on her own shoulders for a decision which may well have implications for the library as a whole. If she feels intimidated she should think first about passing on the request to a colleague who is more senior to her rather than allowing her own insecurities to place the library in a vulnerable position from her decision.

D6.3 A panic out of a crisis?

By just leaving the Director's office without a word to press ahead with the project, Alex is in danger of storing up serious problems for himself. His anger at the Director is merited, but he needs to ensure that he bottles it up for the short term in order to communicate to the Director how flawed his timetable is for implementation. Not saying anything to the Director in this way is as bad as losing his temper with him, since the effect is the same and he does not get the opportunity to offer his professional opinion. If the project is now late then it is likely that Alex will take all the blame.

D6.4 The library snoop

Since Sasha may see this as a storm in a teacup, deleting the e-mail may be tempting. However, there is a management decision that needs to be made here. If Susie's behaviour is beginning to become this erratic it may well be the case that students are noticing it too. It may only be a matter of time before one of the students who are being spied on will complain, at which point it may well come across Sasha's desk again, and with prior knowledge of the behaviour she may well find that her judgement is questioned for not addressing the problem earlier on. Ignoring the situation does not seem sensible in this case.

7

Ethical management of the self, the individual and the organisation

*'I don't need to go on a course, I learned everything
I need to know at library school in 1970!'*

For any profession there are exclusive skills and experiences that will have their own ethical dilemmas. All professionals regardless of their specialty have a body of professional knowledge that they must study and practise before they can be deemed to be professionally competent. However, over and above the professional set of skills learned on the university course that qualifies the student as a professional, there is a set of more generic skills and knowledge that is equally important for professional competency. The previous chapters have dealt with specific ethical issues facing librarians, but this chapter will deal with more common issues that face the professional from any background, namely:

- ethical management of the individual, both of the self and others;
- ethical management of the organisation.

Although this chapter does deal with general issues, like the rest of the book they will be discussed from the point of view of libraries and library professionals.

Management of the self – continuing professional development

Professional skills should be organic; as the knowledge necessary to undertake the job efficiently alters, so should the knowledge of the professional. Undertaking any course that qualifies a person as a professional in any discipline is just the beginning of a journey that should last the lifetime of the career path chosen. Most university courses for professional qualifications offer a body of professional knowledge that allows the recipient to enter that profession. In the case of librarianship many of the courses are accredited by professional associations, and as such need to meet rigorous standards in terms of curriculum and the professional background of the staff members delivering it. The qualification does not give the student the entire knowledge of the profession; this has to come with years of experience building on the scholarly foundation received at library school. Yet atop the library-specific knowledge taught in library schools sit topics such as management and professional development. These issues are just as important to a doctor or a lawyer and reflect the universality of professional competency.

Therefore professional development must be a continuous process. The concept of continuing professional development (CPD) mirrors the ethos of life-long learning which has become prominent from the later decades of the twentieth century. The notion is that, unlike much of the previous fifty years, workers can no longer rely on an unchanging work environment, or even a job for life. To remain employable in the modern world one needs to constantly update skills, especially when part of a profession. This updating can take a variety of forms. As Doney states:

> CPD can be undertaken in a variety of ways. Staff may attend courses, conferences and seminars, study for further qualifications, or simply read the information and library sector literature. Methods of CPD may be formal or informal, individual or as part of a group, in-house or external. (Doney, 1998: 487)

Everything from taking an MBA degree or a PhD to attending a half-day session on changes in copyright law can be deemed to be CPD opportunities. Obviously the level of commitment will vary depending on the nature of CPD chosen, but the emphasis is on learning that is fit for purpose. You may feel at some stage of your career that you require an extra degree to give you a further specialism, for instance in health information or law, but equally you may go through your career picking up everything you need from conferences and the professional literature. No one approach is any better than another but the emphasis has to be on development of the professional knowledge and ensuring that skills remain up to date.

Yet CPD is not something that someone can be forced to do. Even the act of attending a course is a waste of energy and time if the attendee does not listen to what is being taught. One of the authors recalls undertaking a large-scale training programme of library staff that was to be phased over several months, with one session per month that would build on knowledge learned in each previous session. The day after attending the first session a staff member complained that they had not been given notice of their second session yet. It was pointed out to her that insufficient time had elapsed for her to reinforce what she had learned in the first session, but this point seemed to be lost. While being positive about the training opportunity she had received, the staff member seemed to be of the mindset that attending the training was enough, and that no work outside of the training session would be necessary to reinforce what she had learned before she moved on to the next stage.

There have been calls for CPD to become compulsory:

> If we are indeed a profession with our distinct body of competences; if we are proud of that profession and the value that those competences can offer to society; if we are convinced of the need for life-long learning as the basis for maintaining those competences; if we expect a commitment to that life-long learning from our members and are critical of the damage done to the profession by a failure to make that commitment, surely the conclusion has to be a mandatory scheme to ensure that the service to our clients is of the highest possible professional quality. (Noon 1994: 7)

Yet what mechanisms can be put in place to ensure compliance? Not all library associations have formal CPD routes. In the UK CILIP offers two levels of postgraduation qualification, Chartership and Fellowship. Both are only awarded for professionals who have demonstrated a commitment to their professional development. Chartership can be obtained around a year after graduating from an accredited course, while Fellowship can only be applied for after six years and after a demonstrable contribution to the profession can be shown (CILIP, 2006e). Yet while both awards can be revalidated, the revalidation process is not compulsory. This means that those who take their professional development seriously can develop their skills, but it equally means that people can be content with not updating their skills or knowledge.

CPD is not a luxury, it is a necessity. The unwillingness of any professional to update his or her knowledge is a de facto failure to engage with their own indispensable body of knowledge. Few professions have changed to the extent that librarianship has over the past ten years. The impact of technology has transformed how we deliver information to users, and lack of engagement with this key tool can be problematic for librarians. It is also the case that not updating knowledge could mean that bad management decisions could be made. If a professional is unaware of the latest developments in a given area, they may well be making decisions based on inaccurate information. This is when the reluctance to update knowledge becomes more than a personal professional issue, it becomes an organisational one. For instance, consider a librarian who does not keep up to date with copyright law as it pertains to users of library resources. If the law changes and the librarian is not aware of it, he or she could potentially aid a user in breaking the law. This is an extreme example but highlights how old knowledge can be dangerous. Therefore, ethically speaking, management of the self must involve a commitment to the updating of knowledge throughout the length of the career.

Utilising professional networks – discussion lists

Learning to use professional networks sensibly can be a major plus factor in developing a career. Conversely, using them with lack of care and attention could be potentially harmful to a career. One route for keeping up to date is e-mail discussion lists. There are numerous discussion lists for librarians, covering a myriad of topics from general LIS issues to more specialist areas. It can often be tempting when joining one to take part in the professional discussions going on between members – indeed that is what the lists are for. However, it can be easy on such lists to become carried away or get caught up in arguments. On the one hand this is healthy, but on the other hand it can never be accurately estimated how damaging this might be to a career if things get out of hand. For example, if you insult a fellow professional on a discussion list, you never know if you may meet them at some point down the line, or (worst case scenario) if they will be interviewing you for a professional post. Equally, showing ignorance of a topic on such a list can be embarrassing and can also stick in the minds of members. Discussion lists can make the library world seem very small indeed, and it can be surprising how names can become well known for posting to such lists. If such posts are thoughtful and add to the debates this can be a good thing, but if they are lazy, ill-informed and spiteful, this can be detrimental to the professional image of the individual concerned.

Management issues – taking responsibility

Management is about taking decisions. These may be decisions on a micro level, such as deciding on materials to purchase, or on a macro level, such as making serious budgetary decisions regarding opening hours or library closures. Fundamental to the management process, however, is the decision; it is the responsibility that being in a position of authority demands, and it is expected from you by stakeholders from all backgrounds, employees, users or budget holders.

Yet just as selection of materials and delivery of service should be based on unbiased decisions, so too should management decisions. When charged with managing an organisation, a department or an individual, decisions have to be made in the best interests of the service, but the decisions must have grounding in ethical decision-making. Ethical decision-making involves 'honesty, fairness and equity, personal development, respect and integrity' (Bryson, 1999: 130).

Managing change effectively – ethical impossibility?

One of the greatest management challenges is attempting to implement change in an organisation. Change seems to be constant in library and information services, as Gorman has suggested: 'change *is* happening, and more change is coming' (Gorman, 2000: 3). Introducing a new service, altering staff roles, transferring staff to new departments, implementing new technologies, all have potential pitfalls for managers. The literature on change management is extensive and focuses on everything from how to plan change properly to how staff members react to change in an organisation. Roberts and Rowley describe change management in information services as 'the ability to adapt, to redesign structures and services and to continually realign them to stakeholders' needs' (Roberts and Rowley, 2004: 47). This is an important point to remember, as change should not be just about altering something because you feel like it. Equally, it should not be about a service not changing because the staff do not want it to. Changes need to be based on the needs of a modern service, and ideally be evidence-led. It can be tempting, for instance, to see a new service or idea being introduced in another library that gleans a large share of publicity in the professional press and inspires you to make a similar alteration. Unless this is based on evidence of need then it is a risk that may not be worth taking. The politicisation of public services means that increasingly there are funds available for special initiatives for which libraries can bid. It is often the case that library managers feel pressured to bid for such monies in an effort to show that they are forward-thinking and attempting to introduce new levels of service. Attempts to access short-term project funding need to be thought through properly in terms of its need and its potential long-term impact on the service. It can be the case, for instance, that bidding for such funds can lead to staff being removed from their core duties to work on proposals that in the end are unsuccessful. It may be felt that such situations are good opportunities for staff to develop their skills, and this may be the case, but equally if it leads to service detriment in other areas, it needs a clear ethical rationale for the decision.

It could be argued that managing change is an ethical impossibility. Any change will involve a human being who is having his or her condition altered in some way. This may be users who see the service they have happily used for a long time changing in a way they dislike. Or it may be a staff member who is being asked to undertake duties he or she neither wishes to nor has the skills for. Ultimately, even when such changes are made for the organisational good, there may still be people left disappointed or unhappy with the decision, and this will be a situation that will have to be managed positively.

Management of the individual

This brings us to discussion of management of the individual. There are several phrases for this: personnel management, human resources management or people management. All amount to the same thing: how to manage staff in order to get the best out of them, keep them happy in their roles and ensure the organisation benefits. Key to managing staff is the need to build up respect between the staff members and the manager. A reliable indicator as to how well an organisation is being managed is absence rates of staff. If such rates include a large number of stress-related absences then alarm bells should begin to go off in the minds of managers. This may be because a change has been implemented incorrectly or too quickly, or it may be due to bullying or coercive management tactics. Regardless of which it is, the ethical thing for a manager to do is to get to the root of the problem.

Dealing with staff problems needs a manager who is discreet and respectful. It is often the case that as a manager you can become party to sensitive information regarding staff members, especially as this information may relate to health, home life or financial issues. Managers should take great care in handling such information and ensure that the trust between the manager and the staff member is never breached. Similarly, when managing staff performance, the onus should be on a supportive environment and not a punitive one. Winstanley and Stuart-Smith propose four ethical principles that need to be considered when managing performance of staff members:

(1) respect for the individual,
(2) mutual respect,
(3) procedural fairness, and
(4) transparency of decision making. (Winstanley and Stuart-Smith, 1996: 66)

Highlighting these four considerations ensures that all staff members will receive equitable treatment, and there will be no point where consideration of their circumstances will be based on subjective feelings from the manager. This is very important, since if there is any hint that a staff member has been treated unfairly due to personality issues between the manager and the staff member, then this can lead to potential employment tribunal cases. This may ultimately cost the employers if a decisions is found against them.

Conclusion

Management issues, therefore, are a central ethical concern to library and information professionals. While they may not be part of the traditional body of knowledge for librarians, they are vital components of the rounded and responsive professional. Emphasis needs to be on CPD, both for the librarian and their staff. The need to constantly develop and update skills is a central concern for a forward-thinking organisation.

Ethical decision-making needs to be based around the best interests of the organisation and not short-term approaches to problems. Long-term planning involves a reflective and evidence-based approach to service development that introduces changes based only on the proven need for them. By this stance it becomes easier to convince staff and users of the need for the change.

Finally, managing staff needs to be built around respect for them as human beings, with fairness and propriety at the core.

The case studies that follow will discuss some library-based scenarios that illustrate some of the key issues we have discussed above.

Case studies

Case study 7.1 Holiday woes?

David Chivas is a newly qualified librarian who has gained his first professional post as an assistant librarian in a small public library. His line management responsibilities include four library assistants, all of whom have been working there for over five years.

One of his first duties is to draw up a long-term plan for when all of the staff members will be on vacation in the coming year in order to ensure the library is adequately staffed at all times when open. He calls a staff meeting to discuss the vacation slots and then asks for everyone to make their requests to him. One of the assistants, Gillian, says that the first thing that needs to be sorted out is Christmas, as the librarian before David always gave the Christmas vacation period to two of the other assistants who had families, and Gillian feels this is unfair as, although she is childless, she feels that she would like to have Christmas off this year. This then starts a minor squabble between Gillian and one of the other assistants who says that it is selfish of childless people to ask for

Christmas off when she has a family and needs to be at home. Clearly the previous rules have left a lot of resentment between the staff over this issue and David wishes to resolve it before it blows up any further.

David tends to agree with Gillian that to always give the Christmas vacation slots to the same staff members each year is an unreasonable state of affairs, but he also acknowledges that if you have children being with them during Christmas is something you always wish. He can see no way of placating all parties over the issues.

Which of the following decisions should David take?

A David says that he will not be changing the rules of the past, as he would not wish to second-guess the decisions made by the previous librarian who was of long standing. Gillian is angry at this and states that the previous librarian was old-fashioned in attitude and always gave Christmas to families for that reason.
   Go to section A7.1

B David decides to give the vacation slot to Gillian this year because she has not had that slot before. He tells the staff that he will make the decision each year based on staff preferences. This angers the other staff members who feel very much in this case that the person who has complained loudest has received the reward.
   Go to section B7.1

C David says that the only fair way to allocate disputed vacation slots is for lots to be drawn. He tells the staff that no one has the right to the slot as the library is open for large portions of the Christmas period and as such all staff members are potentially contracted to work that period.
   Go to section C7.1

D David decides that the only fair way to allocate the slots is for them to be allocated to two staff members each year from the four, thus every staff member will receive Christmas off every two years.
   Go to section D7.1

Case study 7.2 Stickler for the rules

Dan Furtado is the librarian in charge of a large lending library. One evening shift he is called to one of the counters to handle a complaint by a member of the public who has been demanding change for the photocopier. The library regulations state that change cannot be given for photocopiers as the float allocated to counters is small and is necessary to provide change for users who need to pay fines or purchase some of the value-added services such as DVD or CD borrowing.

When Dan arrives at the counter the staff member who is handling the complaint tells Dan that she cannot give change to the member of the public even if she wanted to as to do so would completely wipe out the float. The member of staff is clearly upset by the exchange with the user, and Dan can see that the user is a particularly rude person who seems to wish to resolve the situation by shouting. The staff member seems ashen-faced and almost close to tears by the encounter.

Dan takes the member of the public aside and explains the situation to him. However, the man becomes even more irate and tells Dan that the staff member and he are being unreasonable and if he does not give change to him he will write a letter of complaint to the local mayor, who happens to be a family friend of his.

How should Dan handle this situation?

A Dan tries to calm the user down but fails to do so. In order to resolve the situation he opens the cash register at the counter and gives the user the change he requires. He tells the user that this is only to resolve the situation and that the rules state that by doing so he is giving the user treatment other people do not get.
   Go to section A7.2

B Dan tells the user that there is no way he can give him change from the cash register and if that he is unhappy with the level of service he should write a letter of complaint and state the nature of his complaint clearly.
   Go to section B7.2

C Dan is unwilling to empty the cash register for the user as it will leave the library staff unable to help users who wish to borrow CDs or DVDs, so he asks the user to wait for 10 minutes while he goes to the library safe to get some more change for the cash register.
   Go to section C7.2

D Dan suggests to the user that in lieu of his behaviour and the way he has treated the member of staff that he should apologise to the staff member or he will be asked to leave the premises.
   Go to section D7.2

Case study 7.3 Old dogs and new tricks?

Paula Parker is the user services librarian in a large university/college library. She has a team that consists of three assistant librarians and ten paraprofessional staff who support the work of the section. Of the three assistant librarians, two have been librarians in the university for over ten years, while one has been a librarian there since he left library school 25 years ago. Bill's responsibility for over 15 years has been user instruction for new students.

As part of an initiative to encourage more efficient use of the library by undergraduate students, Paula's team has been given the responsibility of developing and delivering an information literacy class to all new undergraduate entrants to the university in partnership with the academic practice department. This will be a major undertaking and will involve all of Paula's staff working very hard to deliver the classes.

At a meeting with the three librarians, Paula tells them that they will all need to attend several training classes on information literacy and plagiarism in order to cascade these new concepts to the para-professional staff for delivery to the classes. The meeting does not go well, however. The librarian who has worked at the college for 25 years, Bill, states that this 'new fangled idea' is nonsense and that the user instruction that the library delivers is sufficient for students as it is. Paula is taken aback by this reaction and asks Bill to elaborate on why he thinks the proposal is wrong. Bill sits back and mumbles something under his voice, to which Paula asks him to speak up. Bill then states that he does not need to undergo training in something that he has done for 25 years and that doing so would be a waste of his valuable time.

How should Paula handle this situation?

A Paula quickly calls the meeting to a close and asks Bill to remain behind while she has a word with him. She then proceeds to tell Bill that she will not stand for such insubordination in front of the other staff members, and that if he repeats the behaviour then she will seek to have him disciplined. She tells him that attending the training is not a request, but an order.

 Go to section A7.3

B Paula lets the meeting proceed naturally, and asks Bill to remain behind while she has a word with him. She asks Bill to propose his ideas of how he would deliver this new initiative, since it is a college-wide programme. She listens intently to his ideas and agrees with him that much of what is being proposed is currently being taught, and taught well. She apologises to him for suggesting that what has been done over previous years is in any way deficient, but that as it was the college that had proposed these changes it would be wise to pilot them to see if they could work.

Go to section B7.3

C Paula opens up the meeting to all of the other librarians to see if they share Bill's concerns about the new proposal. They both suggest that what is currently being delivered is very good, and they would have liked to see the college consult the librarians who delivered such courses already before implementing this new initiative.

Go to section C7.3

D Paula suggests that given Bill's interests and experience in the area that he leads on the project, attends a training session on his own with a view to evaluating its effectiveness, and coordinates with the academic practice department with regard to what is to be delivered.

Go to section D7.3

Case study 7.4 There's a way of talking to people!

Amy Grant is a branch librarian in a community library which is part of a network of 12 libraries. One day she is expecting a visit from the area manager, a rather obstreperous man called Mr Tallack who is not highly thought of or respected among the staff.

When Mr Tallack arrives Amy gives him a tour of the facility to let him see how the library is being used and to reinforce to him how busy the branch is. As she is talking to him in the corner of the library she can see him constantly looking over her shoulder at the counter and one of the staff members there. After around a minute of this he suddenly shouts across the room at a staff member that she is taking too long to serve the customer and that there is a queue that needs to be seen to. For a moment Amy cannot quite believe that Mr Tallack has done this in a crowded room with members of the public present.

As Amy and Mr Tallack make their way to her office to conclude their business, Amy can see that the staff member concerned is extremely embarrassed. She makes eye contact with Amy, and it is at this point that Amy wonders if she should say something to Mr Tallack about the inappropriateness of it, or reinforce his rebuke of the staff member instead to curry favour.

How should Amy handle this situation?

A As she passes Amy says to the staff member that Mr Tallack is correct and that she should ensure she does not spend too much time serving customers when there is a queue of people waiting. The staff member becomes even more embarrassed and angry, and the other staff members look at the floor in embarrassment.
   Go to section A7.4

B As she passes the counter Amy states to Mr Tallack that what he did was inappropriate and that to speak to a member of her staff like that, especially in public, was unacceptable. Mr Tallack shouts at Amy and states that he can see where the poor service comes in if that is Amy's attitude.
   Go to section B7.4

C Amy waits until she is back in the office and sitting down before she raises the issue. She tells Mr Tallack that she found the way he spoke to a member of her staff to be unacceptable, and that if he did not offer an apology to the member of staff she would seek to report the incident to the Library Director. Mr Tallack responds by telling her to mind her own business and manage her staff properly instead, but Amy is firm in her argument and tells him that if he wished to he could deliver the apology in secret between him and the staff member, but that she was not willing for him to leave the library without apologising
   Go to section C7.4

D Amy says nothing to Mr Tallack or the staff member and the visit ends. Amy does not mention the incident to any of the staff members again.
   Go to section D7.4

Case study discussions

Sections A7.1 – A7.4

A7.1 Holiday woes?

Not changing the allocation of holidays could seem to the staff like a cowardly decision. Even for those staff that have benefited from the decision it looks to them like David is afraid to make a decision on something as simple as this, and this will be remembered by them for the future. Ultimately, David has taken the easy way out by passing the buck, and this is not a good way to start in a new supervisory role. It is unlikely that any staff member will respect him for this decision.

A7.2 Stickler for the rules?

By handing over the change to the user Dan may well be making the customer happy, but he is letting both the organisation and the staff member down by doing so. The staff member has attempted to carry out library policy for very good reasons, and her adherence to them was for the benefit of the library and users who wished to access value-added services. By giving the user change Dan is undermining the staff member's stance, and this is even worse given the way the user had spoken to the staff member. Understandably the staff member concerned may well feel very upset that Dan has not trusted her judgement and stood by her decision. It is also the case that in the future she may not be as willing to adhere to library policy in the face of a rude user if she feels she will not receive support from her senior colleagues.

A7.3 Old dogs and new tricks?

Understandably Paula is upset that Bill has questioned her judgement over the initiative, but to handle this situation merely by disciplinary action and threats is a rather over-the-top solution. Ultimately Bill's comments come from frustration at not being consulted over the initiative when he is the most knowledgeable member of staff on the topic. Paula needs to consider this and her own insecurities before being able to justify disciplinary procedures.

A7.4 There's a way of talking to people!

Amy's reinforcement of Mr Tallack's rebuke of the member of staff may curry favour with him but it runs the risk of alienating her staff. Amy's motivation to do this was not to address behaviour she found unacceptable, but instead it was an attempt to look forthright in the eyes of her unreasonable supervisor. Given she is reinforcing an already bad decision from him she runs the risk of making herself look as foolish and obstreperous as he is.

Sections B7.1 – B7.4

B7.1 Holiday woes?

By allocating the slot to Gillian, David has made a decision, but in doing so he has made other staff members unhappy. Their feeling that what he has done is to favour the loudest complainer may well also be apt, and may be remembered by other staff members as a tactic for anything they require from him in the future. This may lead to poor supervisor–supervisee relationships in the future.

B7.2 Stickler for the rules?

Dan's decision to back that of his staff member seems entirely appropriate under the circumstances. There really is no need to second-guess the decision as it has been made sensibly under the circumstances. The staff member is very likely to feel better about the incident given Dan's support for her decision-making. While the user may well continue to be irate, he has no right to claim he has been treated unfairly, and his escalated complaint should be of little substance.

B7.3 Old dogs and new tricks?

By seeking a one-on-one meeting with Bill to hear his concerns, Paula is showing her colleague the respect his knowledge and experience merits. Her proposal for Bill to give the initiative a try may well work in this instance, but equally if Bill still considers himself to be out of the loop on a topic area where he has led for 15 years, his resentment about the situation may still remain.

B7.4 There's a way of talking to people!

By letting her staff know that she is unhappy with the way Mr Tallack has spoken to the member of staff, she is supporting her staff publicly, but this may not necessarily be the way to handle the situation given the temperament of Mr Tallack. Amy's motivation here may have been to look good in front of her staff, which is not about solving the problem at hand. The subsequent reaction of Mr Tallack confirms that this may not have been the best way to handle the situation.

Sections C7.1 – C7.4

C7.1 Holiday woes?

Drawing lots seem to be a fair way to handle the situation this year, but it then means coming to this situation again in a year's time. At least in this case David has made a decision and the staff should be able to respect that even while they may not agree with it.

C7.2 Stickler for the rules?

Dan is ensuring that anyone wishing to borrow CDs or DVDs will not be impacted by sourcing change from the library safe, so in that context his decision will not damage other users. However, his decision to give in to the user undermines the decision-making of the staff member who stuck by the rules for the benefit of the library and users. It is quite probable that she will feel aggrieved now, and in the future may not be as willing to adhere to library policy in the face of a rude user.

C7.3 Old dogs and new tricks?

Opening up the meeting to all of the librarians to seek their input is a good way of hearing if Bill's views are held by other staff members. The fact they seemed to confirm his concerns suggests that Paula needs to rethink how she will introduce new initiatives in the future, and ensure that she consults with her staff before making any decisions on implementation.

C7.4 There's a way of talking to people!

By confronting Mr Tallack in private with her concerns she is affording him the respect his status deserves, and she is attempting to resolve the situation with the minimum of fuss. She is well within her rights to make her concerns clear to him, as the branch library is her responsibility. She is also supporting her staff by doing so. She is giving him a respectable way out, and she is also challenging him to think about his behaviour in the future. Given how unreasonable he is, however, he may not take lightly to being forced into an apology and he may remember this incident in the future with bitterness.

Sections D7.1 – D7.4

D7.1 Holiday woes?

Taking turns each so that everyone is guaranteed Christmas off every two years seems to be a fair resolution to the dilemma. The big decision to make would be who gets it that year, but this could be allocated based on lots or on some other mechanism.

D7.2 Stickler for the rules?

By demanding the user apologise to the staff member Dan is placing himself firmly behind her decision-making. In the context of this situation she has done nothing wrong and the user has been unreasonable in his treatment of her, thus she has earned the support of her senior colleague. As much as Dan may have wished to resolve the situation to the satisfaction of all parties, he should not allow a situation to exist that sees his staff members being insulted by a user. This decision is likely to make the staff member feel more empowered in her decision-making, although it may well lead to a complaint about both Dan and the staff member.

D7.3 Old dogs and new tricks?

The strategy to involve Bill in the project is a sensible one, as it will allow him to shape the project based on his professional knowledge and hopefully address his grievances at the same time. It also suggests to the librarians present that Paula trusts them and is willing to listen to their input for initiatives.

D7.4 There's a way of talking to people!

To pretend the incident never happened makes Amy appear weak, both to Mr Tallack and her staff. In both cases they will lose respect for her. Amy also has the big problem of an upset and embarrassed member of staff on her hands.

8

Conclusion – ethical futures

We have discussed a range of ethical principles within this text. At the root of it all has been the goal of excellent service to the library user coupled with ethical responsibility to the organisation, society and the profession.

Within the case studies that support each chapter we have attempted to highlight that there may be more than one response to an ethical dilemma that presents itself. As we stated at the beginning of the book, it is not our intention to second-guess circumstances and tell you which choice you should make for each case study, just as it would be equally inappropriate to do so for someone in their workplace. When facing an ethical dilemma in the workplace, the professional must weigh up in his or her own mind what the best solution is for the specific situation faced. Occasionally the choices made may be forced on you, against your own professional and ethical judgement, by organisational rules or other outside influences. On occasion it may feel like the professional is letting the profession down, but even when a decision may seem like the wrong one, if it is the right one for the organisation then that needs to be considered as an acceptable choice. The competent professional also needs to know when the organisation needs a decision in its favour, even when doing so feels like a challenge to one's personal or professional principles. The classic example of this is the use of Internet filtering in an organisation. It may well be censorship, but equally it may well be expected by the organisation and the user community. You may attempt to lobby them regarding the ethics of the technology, but ultimately having it in place may be an essential component of an organisation's covenant with parents and other stakeholders.

For many ethical dilemmas there is no right or wrong answer. There are options which have specific potential outcomes; some options are more favourable than others based on the ethical principles of the librarian, but there are potentially several acceptable choices that can be made for an ethical dilemma, and not all could be deemed ethically desirable. This does not make them wrong; it merely makes them regrettable from the point of view of the librarian forced into the choice. Compromising one's integrity is a sliding scale. Small compromises may not register much as ethical dilemmas, but the larger the compromise the more the individual needs to question the choice.

The case study chapters that preceded this chapter dealt with a range of potential ethical issues facing librarians. These were grouped into the broad categories of:

- information provision;
- intellectual property questions;
- equity of access and privacy;
- ethical management of the self, the individual and the organisation.

Information provision

The role of the librarian in information provision remains vital and constant. Selection, acquisition, processing, classifying and cataloguing, and finally providing assistance to user access – all are vital cogs in the democratic wheel of providing information to a user. Within this set of processes are ethical dilemmas that we must ensure we understand and manage. Selection must be based solely on the needs of the user community and must not be influenced by outside agencies seeking to block access to the recorded knowledge of humankind. Censorship is a cancer in a civilised society and needs to be fought stringently by librarians. Any attack on intellectual freedom is an attack on the core values of librarianship. As Gorman has observed, 'Librarians believe in intellectual freedom because it as natural to us, and as necessary to us, as the air we breath' (Gorman, 2000: 90).

We must also ensure that the information we provide is of high quality and accurate. In a wired world where misinformation and disinformation collide in a confusing mess for many users, the rational voice needs to be heard, and more often than not for many users it will be the librarian's. This is a vital role in the multimedia world we now inhabit that sees users bombarded with information from television, newspapers, radio and now the Internet. It is a mistake to assume that society has got to grips with the Internet and the challenges it brings in ensuring the information accessed is accurate. In 2004 the BBC found itself embarrassed when it was hoaxed by a campaigner against the company Dow Chemical who had set up a fake website in opposition to them. A researcher attempting to book a Dow employee to comment on the anniversary of the Bhopal chemical disaster stumbled on the site and was convinced of its bona fides. The campaigner was then mistakenly booked for an interview which was carried across several of the BBC's outlets before the hoax was discovered (Wells and Ramesh, 2004).

Intellectual property

Equally, the role of the librarian as protector of recorded knowledge is a vital one. While it is convenient to see copyright and intellectual property as the right of the large corporation to protect its own interests, that is often a simplistic assessment. While the economic aspects of IPR cannot be ignored, the moral rights are just as important. It is unconscionable for a librarian to be party to the breach of intellectual property, but more seriously it is also dangerous for the organisation they serve. The increasing pressure from the Internet generation who see downloading as a way of life means that communicating this message to users may be more difficult than it was 20 years ago, but the message needs to be maintained nonetheless.

At the same time librarians have a moral duty to campaign for IPR that is favourable to users too. The essence of fair dealing is that people are not blocked from copying material for legitimate purposes, normally educational. This is a vital need for a well informed society, and librarians need to ensure that while protecting IPR, they also lobby rights holders to ensure IPR legislation remains fair to all parties. The movement of rights holders towards digital rights management poses enormous ethical challenges. This mechanism for control of intellectual property represents a seismic shift in how information is delivered. The goal is to protect, but it is achieved by restricting access. Certainly as a profession we need to be careful to monitor the usage of DRM software within our service provision to ensure that our emphasis on access is always at the forefront of our thoughts.

Privacy and equity of access

Access to library collections is a fundamental human right. Recognising this is an absolutely vital starting point to any ethical approach to librarianship. Yet equity of access is challenged by several issues, among them geographic obstacles, obstacles of inadequate opening hours and user disabilities. Librarians need to ensure that they continuously challenge barriers to access where they see them, and if such barriers are physical, that they put mechanisms in place to reduce their impact on users. The issue of Internet filtering is an especially controversial area, and while it is clearly a potential barrier to access, it may also be an expected norm for many libraries. In this case librarians need to wrestle with the dilemma of the good of the organisation versus their own ethical values.

Equally the librarian needs to respect the right of the library user to privacy. Even when faced with legislation that attempts to limit such privacy, librarians stand as one of the few professions large enough to lobby against such attempts. Every library user is an individual who deserves respect, as does the personal information the library stores regarding them. In the wired world personal data sets are a commodity and their value needs to be cherished and protected.

Ethical management

Ethical management involves the librarian focusing not just on their organisation, their resources and their staff. An essential component is a focus on their professional competency.

Reflecting on your practice and seeking to identify gaps in knowledge or areas where you could improve that practice are essential components in ensuring that your knowledge remains up to date enough to provide a competent service.

Managing the resources you are trusted with needs skills all of its own. The challenge is to get best use out of what you are given, and ensuring that, even when faced with cuts in finances, the goal is always to provide the best service possible. This can bring numerous ethical challenges, including the appropriate management of change.

When managing staff the focus should be on equality and respect for all staff members. It is not always possible for a professional who is charged with managing staff to be liked and respected by everyone, but when dealing with them there should be no differences in how they are treated. It is also the case that it may well be necessary at some point in a career to make hiring or firing decisions. If so these must be done on the basis of independent decision-making that is for the benefit of the organisation and the users.

The future

The early years of the twenty-first century have been challenging times. The aftermath of the 11 September attacks in the USA has had an enormous impact on the world: an expansion in global conflict and terrorism, a rise in fundamentalism and threats within western states to freedoms and rights that citizens had believed were historic. How will historians of the profession judge librarians of this generation from the point of view of our ethical practice in this challenging era?

The question is a difficult one to answer. If we assume that the liberal values that have defined librarianship since its inception, its focus on equity and privacy, and freedom of thought and expression, continue well into the twenty-first century, then there is a real potential for librarians to be at the forefront of the debate when historic rights are challenged. At the beginning of this book we asked the question whether, in light of the changes in the world and the pressures on freedom of expression and access and privacy, librarians should continue to believe in and fight for the ethical principles that have guided the profession for decades. The answer should be a resounding yes, but with realistic provisos. As Hauptman has stated:

> For a quarter of a century I have maintained that social necessity outweighs professional obligations. I continue to insist that this is the case. Generally, it is possible to fulfil professional mandates without concomitantly sacrificing civil liberties. We do this by making considered and judicious choices. (Hauptman, 2002: 140)

The cases of the John Doe librarians and the British library establishment and their battle over the Terrorism Bill are practical examples of where we can see our ethical beliefs being properly championed. In both instances the librarians involved took a collective responsibility to take on legislation that they felt directly challenged historic rights that citizens had, but also on both occasions the fights were equally about the professional duty of librarians being recognised and respected. The John Doe librarians especially deserve the admiration of all librarians, since their fight was for one of the fundamental values all librarians cherish, that is the right for library users to know their privacy will be respected.

Librarians worldwide need to cherish the principles that have guided them. The ethical principles exist because they are important, and because the communities served by librarians need them to fight these causes for them. The next time anyone suggests to the reader that being a librarian is not really a profession, remind them of the historic freedoms they enjoy and just how important librarians, both individually and collectively, are to their possessing those freedoms. The ethical values of the librarian are the ethical values that knit civilised society together. Attacks on those values either through indifference or design are equally important to take on and win. As Joni Mitchell famously posited:

> 'Don't it always seem to go, you don't know what you've got 'til it's gone'.

In the realm of ethical principles, once they are gone they may never return. All librarians, from library directors to library students, have an equal stake in and responsibility for ensuring those values remain, and are continuously communicated to the profession and the wider world. As Gorman has noted, 'librarianship has a structure and a history, and it behoves librarians to recognize and celebrate their unique identity and mission' (Gorman, 2000: 18).

Librarians should move towards the future not weighed down by the historical ethical principles they have cherished, but feeling empowered by them; they are a vital component of the civilised, rational, reflective and cultured twenty-first century society that the majority of the world craves.

References

ALA (1995) *Code of Ethics of the American Library Association.* Chicago: American Library Association. Available from: *http://www .ala.org/ala/oif/statementspols/codeofethics/codeethics.htm* (last accessed 10 July 2006.

ALA (2006) *Banned Books Week.* Chicago: American Library Association. Available from: *http://www.ala.org/ala/oif/ bannedbooksweek/bannedbooksweek.htm* (last accessed 17 April 2006).

ALIA (2002) *ALIA Core Values Statement.* Available from: *http:// www.alia.org.au/policies/core.values.html* (last accessed 10 July 2006).

ALIA (2005) *Australian Library and Information Association – Statement on Professional Conduct.* Available from: *http://www .alia.org.au/policies/professional.conduct.html* (last accessed 10 July 2006).

Andrews, Sarah (2002) *Privacy and Human Rights 2002: An International Survey of Privacy Laws and Developments.* London: Privacy International. Available from: *http://www .privacyinternational.org/survey/phr2002/* (last accessed 7 July 2006).

Badaracco, C.H. (2002) 'Can book publicity ever be morally neutral?', *Journal of Information Ethics,* 11 (1): 52–6.

BBC News (2005) *Library Sex Surfer Gets Apology.* Available from: *http://news.bbc.co.uk/1/hi/wales/south_east/4356316.stm* (last accessed 7 July 2006).

Bryson, Jo (1999) *Effective Library and Information Centre Management,* 2nd edn. Aldershot: Gower.

CILIP (2005) *Ethical Principles and Code of Professional Practice for Library and Information Professionals.* London: Chartered Institute of Library and Information Professionals. Available from: *http://*

www.cilip.org.uk/professionalguidance/ethics (last accessed 10 July 2006).

CILIP (2006a) *Police and Security Services Have Power to Scrutinise Library Records.* Available from: *http://www.cilip.org.uk/aboutcilip/newsandpressreleases/archive%202005/news051028.htm* (last accessed 12 July 2006).

CILIP (2006b) *The Terrorism Act (2006) received Royal Assent on 30 March 2006.* Available from: *http://www.cilip.org.uk/professionalguidance/terrorismbill* (last accessed 12 July 2006).

CILIP (2006c) *Ethical Principles and Code of Professional Practice for Library and Information Professionals.* Available from: *http://www.cilip.org.uk/professionalguidance/ethics* (last accessed 10 July 2006).

CILIP (2006d) *Terrorism Act 2006.* Available from: *http://www.cilip.org.uk/professionalguidance/terrorismbill/terrorismbill.htm* (last accessed 10 July 2006).

CILIP (2006e) *Framework of Qualifications.* London: Chartered Institute of Library and Information Professionals. Available from: *http://www.cilip.org.uk/qualificationschartership/FrameworkofQualifications* (last accessed 10 July 2006).

CLA (1976) *Position Statements – Code of Ethics.* Ottowa: Canadian Library Association. Available from: *http://www.cla.ca/about/ethics.htm* (last accessed 10 July 2006).

CLA (1985) *Position Statements – Statement on Intellectual Freedom.* Ottowa: Canadian Library Association. Available from: *http://www.cla.ca/about/intfreed.htm* (last accessed 10 July 2006).

Conradi, Mike (2003) 'Liability of an ISP for allowing access to file sharing networks', *Computer Law & Security Report*, 19 (4): 289–94.

DCMS (2005) *Public Libraries: Efficiency and Stock Supply Chain Review.* London: DCMS.

Doney, Elizabeth (1998) 'Developing opinions: the attitude of LIS staff to continuing professional development', *Library Management*, 19 (8): 486–91.

Feather, John (2004) *The Information Society: A Study of Continuity and Change*, 4th edn. London: Facet.

Fernandez-Molina, J. Carlos (2003) 'Laws against the circumvention of copyright technological protection', *Journal of Documentation*, 59 (1): 41–68.

Gorman, Michael (2000) *Our Enduring Values: Librarianship in the 21st Century.* Chicago: American Library Association.

Hannabuss, Stuart (1998) 'Information ethics: a challenge for professionals and the community', *Library Review*, 47 (2): 91–8.

Hannabuss, Stuart (2000) 'Being negligent and liable: a challenge for information professionals', *Library Management*, 21 (6): 316–29.

Hauptman, Robert (1988) *Ethical Challenges in Librarianship*. Phoenix, AZ: Oryx Press.

Hauptman, Robert (2002) *Ethics and Librarianship*. Jefferson, NC and London: McFarland.

IFLA (2000) *Revision of IFLA's Guidelines for Public Libraries*. Amsterdam: International Federation of Library Associations. Available from: *http://www.ifla.org/VII/s8/proj/gpl.htm* (last accessed 7 July 2000).

IFLA (2005) *IFLA/FAIFE Libraries and Intellectual Freedom*. Available from: *http://www.ifla.org/faife/faife/presen.htm* (last accessed 10 July 2006).

IFLA (2006a) *Code of Ethics of the Association of Library and Information Professionals of the Czech Republic*. Available from: *http://www.ifla.org/faife/ethics/czlacode.htm* (last accessed 10 July 2006).

IFLA (2006b) *Code of Ethics of the Association of Indonesian Librarians*. Available from: *http://www.ifla.org/faife/ethics/ipicode.htm* (last accessed 10 July 2006).

IFLA (2006c) *Professional Regulation Commission of the Republic of the Philippines – Code of Ethics for Registered Librarians*. Available from: *http://www.ifla.org/faife/ethics/filicode.htm* (last accessed 10 July 2006).

IFLA (2006d) *Library and Information Association of New Zealand Aotearoa (LIANZA) – Code of Professional Conduct*. Available from: *http://www.ifla.org/faife/ethics/nzcode.htm* (last accessed 10 July 2006).

Joint, Nicholas (2006) 'Teaching intellectual property rights as part of the information literacy syllabus', *Library Review*, 55 (6): 330–6.

Jones, Richard (2005) 'Entertaining code: file sharing, digital rights management regimes, and criminological theories of compliance', *International Review of Law, Computers and Technology*, 19 (3): 287–303.

Koehler, Wallace C. and Pemberton, J. Michael (2000) 'A search for core values: towards a model code of ethics for information professionals', *Journal of Information Ethics*, Spring, 9 (1): 26–54.

Lampert, Lynn D. (2004) 'Integrating discipline based anti-plagiarism instruction into the information literacy curriculum', *Reference Services Review*, 32 (4): 347–55.

Library Journal (2006) 'FBI drops "John Doe" case; librarians say publicity was the key', *Library Journal*, 27 June. Available from: *http://www.libraryjournal.com/article/CA6347404.html* (last accessed 7 July 2006).

Lindsey, Jonathan A. and Prentice, Ann E. (1985) *Professional Ethics in Librarianship*. Phoenix, AZ: Oryx Press.

Loynes, Robert and Proctor, Richard (2000) 'The effect of reduction in public library opening hours on book issues: a statistical analysis', *Journal of Documentation*, 56 (6): 605–23.

Lyman, Peter and Varian, Hal R. (2003) *How Much Information?* Berkeley, CA: School of Information Management and Systems. Available from: *http://www2.sims.berkeley.edu/research/projects/how-much-info-2003/* (last accessed 10 July 2006).

Mendis, Dinusha (2005) 'An insight into the Copyright Licensing Agency and its interaction with higher education institutions', *20th BILETA Conference: Over-Commoditised; Over Centralised; Over-Observed: the New Digital Legal World?* Queen's University of Belfast, April.

Nijboer, Jelke (2004) 'Big Brother versus anonymity on the Internet: implications for Internet service providers, libraries and individuals since 9/11', *New Library World*, 105 (1202–3): 256–61.

Noon, Patrick (1994) 'CPD: professional development – continuing and compulsory?', *Librarian Career Development*, 2 (4): 4–8.

O'Sullivan, Connie and O'Sullivan, Michael (2005) 'Monkey business: the intelligent design war has come to the school library', *School Library Journal*, 1 November. Available from: *http://www.schoollibraryjournal.com/article/CA6277831.html* (last accessed 17 April 2006).

Oder, Norman (2005) '9/11 hijackers used other library', *Library Journal*, 1 June. Available from: *http://www.libraryjournal.com/article/CA602668.html* (last accessed 10 July 2006.

Overdrive (2003) *Top Libraries Select Overdrive eBooks System*. Available from: *http://www.overdrive.com/news/pr/12162003.asp* (last accessed 10 July 2006).

Ranganathan, S.R. (1931) *The Five Laws of Library Science*. Madras: Madras Library Association.

Resnick, Paul J., Hansen, Derek L. and Richardson, Caroline R. (2004) 'Calculating error rates for filtering software: establishing a blueprint for conducting and reporting tests of filter effectiveness', *Communications of the ACM*, 47 (9): 67–71.

Roberts, Sue and Rowley, Jennifer (2004) *Managing Information Services*. London: Facet.

Sign and Sight (2006) *The Twelve Muhammed Cartoons: A Survey of the European Press.* Available from: *http://www.signandsight.com/features/590.html* (last accessed 7 July 2006).

SLIS (2001) *Copyright Resources.* School of Library and Information Science, University of North Texas. Available from: *http://web2.unt.edu/children/copyright/list.cfm* (last accessed 10 July 2006).

Smith, Gregory A. (ed.) (2002) *Christian Librarianship: Essays on the Integration of Faith and Profession.* Jefferson, NC and London: McFarland.

Sturges, Paul (2002) *Public Internet Access in Libraries and Information Centres.* London: Facet.

Sturges, Paul (2003) 'Doing the right thing: professional ethics for information workers in Britain', *New Library World*, 104 (1186): 94–102.

University of Central England (1999) *Mapplethorpe Book Provokes Academic Freedom Dispute.* Available from: *http://www.uce.ac.uk/mapplethorpe/* (last accessed 7 July 2006).

Wells, Matt and Ramesh, Randeep (2004) 'BBC reputation hit by Bhopal interview hoax', *Guardian Online*, 4 December. Available from: *http://media.guardian.co.uk/site/story/0,14173,1366411,00.html* (last accessed 10 July 2006).

Winstanley, Diana and Stuart-Smith, Kate (1996) 'Policing performance: the ethics of performance management', *Personnel Review*, 25 (6): 66–84.

Suggested readings
on ethics in librarianship

These readings should offer those interested in taking some of the topics further a broad range of materials. They are based on material cited in the chapters plus other materials of relevance to ethical issues.

Books

Foskett, D.J. (1962) *The Creed of a Librarian: No Politics, No Religion, No Morals*. London: Library Association.

Gorman, Michael (2000) *Our Enduring Values: Librarianship in the 21st Century*. Chicago: American Library Association.

Hauptman, Robert (1988) *Ethical Challenges in Librarianship*. Phoenix, AZ: Oryx Press.

Hauptman, Robert (2002) *Ethics and Librarianship*. Jefferson, NC and London: McFarland.

Lindsey, Jonathan A. and Prentice, Ann E. (1985) *Professional Ethics in Librarianship*. Phoenix, AZ: Oryx Press.

Mason, Richard O., Mason, Florence M. and Culnan, Mary J. (1995) *Ethics of Information Management*. Thousand Oaks, CA and London: Sage.

Ranganathan, S.R. (1931) *The Five Laws of Library Science*. Madras: Madras Library Association.

Smith, Gregory A. (ed.) (2002) *Christian Librarianship: Essays on the Integration of Faith and Profession*. Jefferson, NC and London: McFarland.

Sturges, Paul (2002) *Public Internet Access in Libraries and Information Centres*. London: Facet.

Journal articles

Adams, M. (1999) 'Preserving rights in the information age', *Library Issues: Briefings for Faculty and Adminstrators,* 19 (5): 1–3.

Alfino, M. and Pierce, L. (2001) 'The social nature of information', *Library Trends,* 49 (3): 471–85.

Allen, B., Maloney, K., Morden, D. and Stoffle, C.J. (2003) Continuing to build the future: academic libraries and their challenges', *Portal: Libraries and the Academy,* 3 (3): 363–80.

Allen, G. (1998) 'Work values in librarianship', *Library and Information Science Research,* 20 (4): 415–24.

Anderson, R.E. and Dill, B.J. (2003) 'Ethics-related technology policies in schools', *Social Science Computer Review,* 21 (3): 326–39.

Angel, C. (2000) 'The right to privacy', *Journal of Information Ethics,* 9 (2): 11–25.

Auer, N.J. and Krupar, E.M. (2001) 'Mouse click plagiarism: the role of technology in plagiarism and the librarian's role in combating it', *Library Trends,* 49 (3): 415–32.

Austin, B. (2004) 'Should there be "privilege" in the relationship between reference librarian and patron?', *Reference Librarian,* 87/88: 301–11.

Badaracco, C.H. (2002) 'Can book publicity ever be morally neutral?', *Journal of Information Ethics,* 11 (1): 52–6.

Bailey, R.L. (1997) 'Information: the currency of the new millennium', *International Information and Library Review,* 29 (3–4): 319–31.

Beghtol, C. (2002) 'A proposed ethical warrant for global knowledge representation and organization systems', *Journal of Documentation,* 58 (5): 507–32.

Beghtol, C. (2005) 'Ethical decision-making for knowledge representation and organization systems for global use', *Journal of the American Society for Information Science and Technology,* 56 (9): 903–12.

Benedict, K. (2004) 'Ethics and the archival profession: introduction and case studies', *Archives and Manuscripts,* 32 (1): 143–4.

Blanke, H.T. (1996) 'Librarianship and public culture in the age of information capitalism', *Journal of Information Ethics,* 5 (2): 54–69.

Bodi, S. (1998) 'Ethics and information technology: some principles to guide students', *Journal of Academic Librarianship,* 24 (6): 459–63.

Britz, J.J. (2003) 'Info: a critical re-evaluation with special reference to implications for information ethics', *Mousaion,* 21 (1): 53–81.

Britz, J.J. (2004) 'To know or not to know: a moral reflection on information poverty', *Journal of Information Science*, 30 (3): 192–204.

Britz, J.J. and Blignaut, J.N. (2001) 'Information poverty and social justice', *South African Journal of Library and Information Science*, 67 (2): 63–9.

Buchanan, E.A. (1996) 'Ethical transformations in a global information age', *Technical Services Quarterly*, 13 (3/4): 23–38.

Buchanan, E.A. (2004) 'Ethics in library and information science: what are we teaching?', *Journal of Information Ethics*, 13 (1): 51–60.

Bunge, C.A. (1999) 'Ethics and the reference librarian', *Reference Librarian*, 66: 25–43.

Burbules, N.C. (2001) 'Paradoxes of the Web: the ethical dimensions of credibility', *Library Trends*, 49 (3): 441–53.

Buschman, J. and Rosenzweig, M. (1999) 'Intellectual freedom within the library workplace: an exploratory study in the US', *Journal of Information Ethics*, 8 (2): 36–45.

Campbell, L.M. (2000) 'Keeping watch on the waterfront: social responsibility in legal and library professional organizations', *Law Library Journal*, 92 (3): 263–86.

Carbo, T. and Almagno, S. (2001) 'Information ethics: the duty, privilege and challenge of educating information professionals', *Library Trends*, 49 (3): 510–18.

Carlin, A.P. (2003) 'Disciplinary debates and bases of interdisciplinary studies: the place of research ethics in library and information science', *Library and Information Science Research*, 25 (1): 3–18.

Carney, S.M. (2003) 'Democratic communication and the library workplace', *Journal of Information Ethics*, 12 (2): 43–59.

Carr, M.M. and Greever, B.C. (1995) 'The margin of victory: how the Idaho Library Association defeated an antigay initiative', *Library Journal*, 120 (14): 136–9.

Chapin, B. (1999) 'The comfortable pew is a thorny throne', *Teacher Librarian: The Journal for School Library Professionals*, 26 (5): 18–22.

Chepaitis, E. (2000) 'The criticality of information ethics in emerging economies: beyond piracy and privacy', *Journal of Information Ethics*, 9 (2): 5–7.

Choi, K.Y. and Chow, W.S. (2003) 'Identifying managers who need ethics training in using IT at work', *Behaviour and Information Technology*, 22 (2): 117–25.

Cline, E. (1995) 'Here comes a chopper to chop off your head: freedom of expression versus censorship in America', *Journal of Information Ethics*, 4 (2): 18–32.

Contreras, S. and Jefferson, R.N. (2005) 'Ethical perspectives of library and information science graduate students in the United States', *New Library World*, 106 (1): 58–66.

Cornog, M. and Perper, T. (1997) 'For sex, see librarian: a plague on both your houses? The other sex books', *Journal of Information Ethics*, 6 (1): 8–12.

Cottrell, J.R. (1999) 'Ethics in an age of changing technology: familiar territory or new frontiers?', *Library Hi Tech*, 17 (1): 107–13.

Cox, J. (1996) 'Copyright: economic rights and moral rights', *Acquisitions Librarian*, 15: 123–8.

Cox, P. (1997) 'The conceits of law and the transmission of the indecent, obscene, and ugly', *Journal of Information Ethics*, 6 (2): 23–34.

Cox, R.J. (2001) 'Testing the spirit of the Information Age', *Journal of Information Ethics*, 10 (2): 51–66.

Danielson, E.S. (1997) 'Ethics and reference services', *Reference Librarian*, 56: 107–24.

Davies, B. and Curry, A. (2001) 'Literature about illicit drugs: libraries and the law', *Journal of Information Ethics*, 10 (2): 13–37.

De Parga, M.V. (1997) 'Electronic records and the memory of our time', *International Information and Library Review*, 29 (3–4): 299–305.

Decew, J.W. (1998) 'In pursuit of privacy: law, ethics and the rise of technology', *Journal of Government Information*, 25 (3): 307–8.

Devlin, M. and Miller, H. (1995) 'Ethics in action: the vendor's perspective', *Serials Librarian*, 25 (3/4): 295–300.

Diamond, R. and Dragich, M. (2001) 'Professionalism in librarianship: shifting the focus from malpractice to good practice', *Library Trends*, 49 (3): 395–414.

Dilevko, J. (1999) 'Why Sally Tisdale is really upset about the state of libraries: socio-political implications of Internet information sources', *Journal of Information Ethics*, 8 (1): 37–62.

Dole, W.V. and Hurych, J.M. (2001) 'Values for librarians in the information age', *Journal of Information Ethics*, 10 (2): 38–50.

Dole, W.V., Hurych, J.M. and Koehler, W.C. (2000) 'Values for librarians in the information age: an expanded examination', *Library Management*, 21 (6 and 7): 285–97.

Dowell, D.R. (2003) 'Who should be allowed to touch the patron?', *Library Mosaics*, 14 (2): 8–9.

Doyle, T. (1998) 'A Millian critique of library censorship', *Journal of Academic Librarianship*, 24 (3): 241–3.

Doyle, T. (2001) 'A utilitarian case for intellectual freedom in libraries', *Library Quarterly*, 71 (1): 44–71.

Doyle, T. (2004) 'Should web sites for bomb making be legal?', *Journal of Information Ethics*, 13 (1): 34–7.

Eisenman, R. (2000) 'Incompetence: more prevalent than many realize', *Journal of Information Ethics*, 9 (1): 5–9.

Eisenman, R. (2001) 'Child molesters on the Internet: how they lure children', *Journal of Information Ethics*, 10 (1): 73–8.

Ercegovak, Z. and Richardson, J.V. (2004) 'Academic dishonesty, plagiarism included, in the digital age: a literature review', *College and Research Libraries*, 65 (4): 301–18.

Erdelez, S. and Houston, R.D. (2004) 'The digital divide: who really benefits from the proposed solutions for closing the gap', *Journal of Information Ethics*, 13 (1): 19–33.

Etzioni, A. (1997) 'The First Amendment is not an absolute even on the Internet', *Journal of Information Ethics*, 6 (2): 64–6.

Falk, Howard (2004) 'Privacy in libraries', *Electronic Library*, 22 (3): 281–4.

Flowers, J.L. (2002) 'Ethics within the serials family', *Library Collections, Acquisitions, and Technical Services*, 26 (4): 449–56.

Frazier, K. (1999) 'Collection development and professional ethics', *Journal of Library Administration*, 28 (1): 33–46.

Freeman, M. (1996) 'Living by the code: some issues surrounding a code of conduct for the LIS profession', *New Library World*, 97 (1129): 17–21.

Fricke, M., Mathiesen, K. and Fallis, D. (2000) 'The ethical presuppositions behind the Library Bill of Rights', *Library Quarterly*, 70 (4): 468–489.

Froehlich, T.J. (1998) 'Ethical considerations regarding library nonprofessionals: competing perspectives and values', *Library Trends*, 46 (3): 444–66.

Gannon-Leary, P. (1997) '"E" for exposed? E-mail and privacy issues', *Electronic Library*, 15 (3): 221–6.

Geiszler, R.W. (1998) 'Patron behavior policies in the public library', *Journal of Information Ethics*, 7 (1): 54–67.

Genieva, E. (1997) 'Legal aspects of the Internet', *International Information and Library Review*, 29 (3–4): 381–92.

Ghonaimy, M.A.R. (1997) 'Existing and evolving technologies for long-term information preservation and the supporting legal requirements', *International Information and Library Review*, 29 (3–4): 367–79.

Gorniak-Kocikowska, K. (2001) 'Revolution and the library', *Library Trends*, 49 (3): 454–70.

Gosseries, A. (2003) 'A case for restricted access', *Journal of Information Ethics*, 12 (1): 56–66.

Graybosch, A.J. (2001) 'Bootlegs: intellectual property and popular culture', *Journal of Information Ethics*, 10 (1): 35–50.

Grupe, F. (2003) 'Information systems professionals and conflict of interest', *Information Management and Computer Security*, 11 (1): 28–32.

Hamilton, N.W. (2003) 'Academic ethics problems and materials on professional conduct and shared governance', *Journal of Academic Librarianship*, 29 (6): 416–17.

Hannabuss, S. (1996) 'Teaching library and information ethics', *Library Management*, 17 (2): 24–35.

Hannabuss, S. (1998) Information ethics: a contemporary challenge for professionals and the community', *Library Review*, 47 (1 and 2): 91–8.

Hannabuss, S. (2000) 'Being negligent and liable: a challenge for information professionals', *Library Management*, 21 (6 and 7): 316–29.

Henderson, A. (1998) 'The ethics of the library crisis and the First Amendment', *Publishing Research Quarterly*, 4: 31–40.

Hauptman, R. (2001) 'Technological implementations and ethical failures', *Library Trends*, 49 (3): 433–40.

Highby, W. (2004) 'The ethics of academic collection development in a politically contentious era', *Library Collections, Acquisitions, & Technical Services*, 28 (4): 465–72.

Hill, M.W. (1998) 'Facing up to dilemmas: conflicting ethics and the modern information professional', *Aslib Proceedings*, 50 (4): 71–8.

Holm, S. and Vaagan, R. (2004) 'Professional values in Norwegian librarianship', *New Library World*, 105 (5): 213–17.

Holverstott-Cockrell, M. (1998) 'The need for information ethics: a graduate student's perspective', *Library and Archival Security*, 14 (2): 67–73.

Hsu, M. and Kuo, F. (2003) 'An investigation of volitional control in information ethics', *Behaviour and Information Technology*, 22 (1): 53–62.

Iaccarino, G. (1996) 'A look at Internet privacy and security issues and their relationship to the electronic job search: implications for librarians and career services professionals', *Reference Librarian*, 55: 107–13.

Iacovino, L. (2002) 'Ethical principles and information professionals: theory, practice and education', *Australian Academic and Research Libraries*, 33 (2): 57–74.

Inoue, H., Naito, E. and Koshizuka, M. (1997) 'Mediacy: what it is? Where to go?', *International Information and Library Review*, 29 (3–4): 403–13.

Jaeger, J. (1999) 'User fees, community goods, and the public library', *Public Library Quarterly*, 17 (2): 49–62.

Janssen, A. (2000) 'Freedom of speech, sexual harassment, and Internet filters in academic libraries', *Journal of Information Ethics*, 9 (2): 37–45.

Jayasundara, C.C. (2004) 'Ethical issues surrounding the use of information in health care', *Malaysian Journal of Library and Information Science*, 9 (1): 69–80.

John, N.R. (2000) 'The ethics of the click: users and digital information in the Internet age', *Libri*, 50 (2): 129–35.

Jones, B. (2001) 'Narrative identity as a central theme in an ethics of librarianship', *Australian Library Journal*, 50 (2): 121–31.

Juznic, P., Urbanija, J., Grabrijan, E., Miklavc, S., Oslaj, D. and Svoljsak, S. (2001) 'Excuse me, how do I commit suicide? Access to ethically disputed items of information in public libraries', *Library Management*, 22 (1/2): 75–9.

Ketelaar, E. (1995) 'The right to know, the right to forget? Personal information in public archives', *Archives and Manuscripts*, 23 (1): 8–17.

Ketelaar, E. (1997) 'Can we trust information?', *International Information and Library Review*, 29 (3–4): 333–8.

Kilcullen, M. and Kooistra, J.O. (1999) 'At least do no harm: sources on the changing role of business ethics and corporate social responsibility', *Reference Services Review*, 27 (2): 158–78.

Kim, Y. (1999) 'Critical IS issues in the networked era', *Information Resources Management Journal*, 12 (4): 14–23.

Knuth, R. (1996) 'Through the lens of theory: perspectives on an international library association', *International Information and Library Review*, 28 (4): 303–29.

Koehler, W.C. and Pemberton, J.M. (2000) 'A search for core values: towards a model code of ethics for information professionals', *Journal of Information Ethics*, 9 (1): 26–54.

Koomen, K. (1997) 'The Internet and international regulatory issues', *International Information and Library Review*, 29 (3–4): 271–97.

Kulikowski, J. (1997) 'Open access to information highways: chances and dangers for developing countries', *International Information and Library Review*, 29 (2): 181–8.

Kurland, N.B. (1996) 'Engendering democratic participation via the Net: access, voice, and dialogue', *Information Society*, 12 (4): 387–406.

Laidlaw-Johnson, E.A. (1996) 'The ethics of information transfer in the electronic age: scholars unite!', *Journal of Information Ethics*, 5 (2): 29–38.

Lampert, L.D. (2004) 'Integrating discipline-based anti-plagiarism instruction into the information literacy curriculum', *Reference Services Review*, 32 (4): 347–55.

Leary, M.A. (2003) 'Service: the core of law librarianship', *Legal Reference Services Quarterly*, 22 (4): 1–10.

Li, J.H. (2000) 'The death of privacy: the lively debate in *The Washington Post* (1974–1998)', *Journal of Information Ethics*, 9 (1): 63–88.

Lorenzen, E.A. (1996) 'The librarian's role in the job search of the future: issues and ethics in the electronic environment', *Reference Librarian*, 55: 1–6.

Lorenzo, P. (1995) 'Answering legal questions at the reference desk: issues of ethics, liability, and use of legal collections', *Current Studies in Librarianship*, 19 (1/2): 13–23.

Luey, B. (1996) 'The librarian's role in teaching academic authors about publishing procedures and ethics', *Serials Review*, 22 (1): 39–46.

Manna, D.R. and Smith, A.D. (2004) 'Exploring the trust factor in e-medicine', *Online Information Review*, 28 (5): 346–55.

Marco, G.A. (1995) 'Two false dogmas of censorship', *New Library World*, 96 (1124): 15–19.

Marco, G.A. (1996) 'Ethics for librarians: a narrow view', *Journal of Librarianship and Information Science*, 28 (1): 33–8.

Marcum, D. (1997) 'A moral and legal obligation: preservation in the digital age', *International Information and Library Review*, 29 (3–4): 357–65.

Mazikana, P. (1997) 'The challenges of archiving digital information', *International Information and Library Review*, 29 (3–4): 307–17.

McCaskie, R. (1999) 'Corporate governance, decision making and evidence: an information management perspective', *Records Management Journal*, 9 (2): 75–91.

Miltenhoff, Plamen and Hauptman, Robert (2005) 'Ethical dilemmas in libraries: an international perspective', *Electronic Library*, 23 (6): 664–70.

Moran, G. (2001) 'Ethics, strengths and values: a review article', *Journal of Librarianship and Information Science*, 33 (2): 98–101.

Moran, J. and Taylor, M. (2003) 'Lowering the drawbridge: further thoughts on discriminating between readers', *Journal of the Society of Archivists*, 24 (1): 55–64.

Mumford, E. (1995) 'Technology and freedom: hope or reality', *Information Services and Use*, 15 (1): 3–24.

Myers, B. (2004) 'Safekeeping the public trust: librarians and fundraisers in partnership', *Bottom Line*, 17 (1): 31–3.

Nalen, J.E. (2001) 'Institute for Global Ethics', *Journal of Business and Finance Librarianship*, 6 (4): 73–8.

Nijboer, J. (2004) 'Big Brother versus anonymity on the Internet: implications for Internet service providers, libraries and individuals since 9/11', *New Library World*, 105 (1202–3): 256–61.

Oberg, L.R. and Kirk, M.L. (1995) 'Banned books, politics and ethics: a conversation between Larry Oberg and Maresa L. Kirk', *Library Mosaics*, 6 (4): 10–13.

O'Neil, R.M. (1998) 'Free speech in cyberspace', *Journal of Information Ethics*, 7 (1): 15–23.

Oppenheim, C. and Pollecutt, N. (2000) 'Professional associations and ethical issues in LIS', *Journal of Librarianship and Information Science*, 32 (4): 187–203.

O'Shea, A. (2004) 'Under threat: libraries in Iraq', *Library Mosaics*, 15 (4): 14–17.

O'Toole, J. (2004) 'Archives and historical accountability: toward a moral theology of archives', *Archivaria*, 58: 3–20.

Palmer, S.S. (1999) 'Reference service: what makes it good? What makes it ethical?', *Journal of Information Ethics*, 8 (2): 46–58.

Peace, A.G. (1997) 'Academia, censorship, and the Internet', *Journal of Information Ethics*, 6 (2): 35–47.

Prior, M., Rogerson, S. and Fairweather, B. (2002) 'The ethical attitudes of information systems professionals: outcomes of an initial survey', *Telematics and Informatics*, 19 (1): 21–36.

Prochaska, A. (2003) 'Are we all global librarians now?', *Journal of Library Administration*, 39 (4): 79–88.

Richmond, L.D. (2003) 'The pro se patron: an ethical rather than legal dilemma', *Legal Reference Services Quarterly*, 22 (2/3): 75–84.

Rockenbach, B. (1998) 'Information ethics at the University of Pittsburgh', *Journal of Information Ethics*, 7 (2): 13–18.

Rockenbach, B. (2000) 'Image ethics: security and manipulation of digital images', *Journal of Information Ethics*, 9 (2): 66–71.

Ross, L. (2000) 'Internet selection software and the acquisition/removal distinction', *Journal of Information Ethics*, 9 (2): 46–50.

Rumbough, T. (2003) 'Explosive information: how the Internet can help terrorists', *Journal of Information Ethics*, 12 (2): 16–30.

Saksida, M. (1997) 'The information society in the twenty first century: converting from analogue to digital', *International Information and Library Review*, 29 (3–4): 261–7.

Schweinsburg, J.D. (1997) 'Family Friendly Libraries versus the American Library Association: a test of democracy', *Journal of Information Ethics*, 6 (2): 75–87.

Seadle, M. (2002) 'Copyright in the networked world: moral rights', *Library Hi Tech*, 20 (1): 124–7.

Seadle, M. (2004) 'Copyright in a networked world: ethics and infringement', *Library Hi Tech*, 22 (1): 106–10.

Sha, Y. (2004) 'On the 4-dimensional theoretical framework of information ethics', *Journal of the China Society for Scientific and Technical Information*, 23 (4): 484–9.

Singleton, A. (2003) 'Terrorism, the publishing decision and beyond', *Learned Publishing*, 16 (3): 189–92.

Smith, M. (2001) 'Global information justice: rights, responsibilities, and caring connections', *Library Trends*, 49 (3): 519–37.

Smith, M.M. (2003) 'Walking with the FBI: patriotism as personal dissent 1 year after 9 /11', *Journal of Information Ethics*, 12 (2): 10–15.

Sturges, P. (2003) 'Doing the right thing: professional ethics for information workers in Britain', *New Library World*, 104 (3): 94–102.

Tavani, H. (2000) 'Privacy enhancing technologies as a panacea for online privacy concerns: some ethical considerations', *Journal of Information Ethics*, 9 (2): 26–36.

Taylor, J.K. (1997) 'Protecting minors from free speech', *Journal of Information Ethics*, 6 (2): 67–74.

Taylor, M. (2001) 'Patients' rights on the World Wide Web', *Medical Reference Services Quarterly*, 20 (2): 57–70.

Tirimanne, N. (2001) 'The ethics of information provision: a case for refugees', *Journal of Information Ethics*, 10 (2): 67–73.

Trushina, I. (2004) 'Freedom of access: ethical dilemmas for Internet librarians', *Electronic Library*, 22 (5): 416–21.

Vaagan, R.W. (2003) 'LIS education: repackaging infopreneurs or promoting value-based skills?', *New Library World*, 104 (4/5): 156–63.

Vaagan, R. and Koehler, W. (2005) 'Intellectual property rights vs. public access rights: ethical aspects of the DeCSS decryption program', *Information Research*, 10 (3). Available from: *http://informationr.net/ir/10-3/paper230.html*.

Van Buren, C. (2001) 'Teaching hackers: school computing culture and the future of cyber-rights', *Journal of Information Ethics*, 10 (1): 51–72.

Ward, P.L. (2000) 'Trends in library management', *Library Review*, 49 (8 and 9): 436–41.

Wengert, R.G. (2001) *Ethical Issues in Information Technology*, Special Issue of *Library Trends*, 49 (3): 391–537.

Wengert, R.G. (2001) 'Some ethical aspects of being an information professional', *Library Trends*, 49 (3): 486–509.

Winston, M. (2005) 'Ethical leadership: professional challenges and the role of LIS education', *New Library World*, 106 (5): 234–43.

Young, S. (1997) 'Sexually-explicit materials via the Internet: ethical concerns for the library profession', *Journal of Academic Librarianship*, 23 (1): 49–50.

Yusuf, M. (1997) 'Reliability and accountability of digital information through time', *International Information and Library Review*, 29 (3–4): 339–55.

Index

academic:
    librarians, 7
    libraries, 43, 87
acceptable use policies, 13, 91–2
access to information, 4, 5,
    16–21, 31, 34, 35, 48–52,
    85–9, 128
ALA – *see* American Library
    Association
ALIA – *see* Australian Library
    and Information Association
American Library Association, 8,
    49
    ethical code, 29–31
Association for Indonesian
    Librarians:
    ethical code, 36–7
Association of Library and
    Information Professionals of
    the Czech Republic:
    ethical code, 34–6
AUPs – *see* acceptable use policies
Australia, 39–40
Australian Library and
    Information Association, 86
    ethical code, 39–40
ATMs, 3

banned books, 49
BBC, 127
BPI – *see* British Phonographic
    Industry

Bhopal, 127
Birmingham, 14
BL – *see* British Library
blogs, 2
bomb making, xiii, 3, 14,
    35
Bond, Henry, 22
books, 4, 21
    banned, 49
    lending, 7, 9
    promotion, 44
British Broadcasting Corporation
    – *see* BBC
British Library, 95
British Phonographic Industry,
    69

calendars, 3
California, 72
camcorders, 2
Canada, 31–2
Canadian Library Association:
    ethical code, 31–2
Carnegie, Andrew, 88
cartoons, 19, 49
case studies, xiv, 52–63, 74–84,
    96–106, 114–24
cataloguers, 46–8
cataloguing, 4–5, 46–8
CDs, 21, 69, 71
censorship, 16, 19–20, 29, 35, 38,
    49, 126

Chartered Institute of Library and
Information Professionals, 9,
10, 95
  Chartership, 109–10
  ethical code, 32–4, 86
  Fellowship, 109–10
chat, 2, 13
chemicals, 3
children, 20, 48–9, 91
CLA – *see* Canadian Library
Association or Copyright
Licensing Agency
classification, 4–5, 46–8
'Clause 28', 12
conferences, 109
conferencing (Internet), 2
confidentiality, 90
Connecticut, 9, 10, 95
continuous professional
development – *see* librarians,
professionalism
copyright – *see* intellectual
property
Copyright Licensing Agency, 66, 67
corporate librarians, 7
course packs, 67–8
CPD – *see* librarians,
professionalism
creationism, 30, 47
Czech Republic, 34–6

data protection, 92–4
Data Protection Act 1984, 93
Data Protection Act 1998, 93
DDC – *see* Dewey Decimal
Classification
democracy, 16, 19, 34
developing world, 87
Dewey Decimal Classification,
46–8
Dewey, Melvil, 48

digital rights management, 70–1,
73, 127
Disabilities Act 1990, 88
Disability Discrimination Act
1995, 88
discrimination, 40
discussion lists, 110–11
Dover School District,
Pennsylvania, 47
Dow Chemical, 127
downloading, 22, 69, 127
DRM – *see* digital rights
management
DVDs, 2, 21, 71

easyinternetnetcafe, 69
eBooks, 71
economic commodities, 2, 90
e-mail, 2
embezzlement, 22
employment tribunals, 113
encryption, 3
environment, 2
ethics, xiii–xv, 1, 7, 9, 27, 125–35
  case studies, xiv, 52–63, 74–84,
96–106, 114–24
  codes, xiv, 8, 13, 27–41
  organisational management,
11, 12, 17, 22–4, 31,
107–14, 128
  personal, xiii, 11
  public, xiii
  principles, 13, 27
  social norms, 11, 14
  standards, 8
  taxonomies, 1–5
  teaching, xiii

FAIFE – *see* Free Access to
Information and Freedom of
Expression

fair dealing, 66, 70, 127
fiction, 44
file sharing, 69
films, 2
filtering, 18, 20, 91–2, 125, 127
Florida, 94
Free Access to Information and
    Freedom of Expression, 87
free speech, 50

gatekeeping, 17–18, 20–2, 73
Glasgow, 27
Google, 50
Gorman, Michael, 10–11, 16,
    20, 85, 86, 92, 111, 126,
    130
government, 23, 37, 39, 90, 93

Hannabuss, Stuart, 51
Hauptman, Robert, xiii, 6, 14–15,
    20, 35, 91, 129
Hippocratic Oath, 15
homosexuality, 12
Huckleberry Finn (novel), 49

identity cards, 93
IFLA, 87
inappropriate materials, 20–1
industries:
    oil, 12
    pharmaceutical, 12
information:
    access, 4, 5, 16–21, 31, 34, 35,
        48–52, 85–9, 128
    cataloguing and classification,
        4–5, 46–8
    case studies, 52–63, 74–84,
        96–106, 114–24
    definitions, 2–5
    literacy, 51
    personal, 3, 5

privacy, 10, 17–21, 30, 89–95,
    128
purchasing, 23, 45–6
selection, 43–4, 126–7
value, 3
intellectual:
freedom, 16, 19, 31, 39, 126
property, 2, 17, 21–2, 30, 35,
    39, 65–73, 127
intelligent design – *see*
    creationism
International Federation of
    Library Associations – *see*
    IFLA
Internet, 2, 3, 9, 50–1, 125–6
    acceptable use policies, 13,
        91–2
    access, 10, 27
    blogs, 2
    chat, 2, 13
    conferencing, 2
    discussion lists, 110–11
    e-mail, 2
    filtering, 18, 20, 91–2, 125,
        127
    privacy, 93–4
    spam, 90
    web pages, 2, 4
    webcams, 2
iPods, 70
IPR – *see* intellectual property
iTunes, 70

John Does, 9–10, 11, 94–5,
    129–30

laws, xiii, 1, 9–10, 12, 69, 88, 93,
    94–5, 129
    unethical, 10
learning, 7, 24
    lifelong, 23, 87

lending books, 7, 9
LIANZA – see Library
    Association of New Zealand
    Aotearoa
librarians:
    academic, 7
    case studies, 52–63, 74–84,
        96–106, 114–24
    cataloguers, 46–8
    corporate, 7
    ethical influences, 11–25,
        27–41, 125–30
    gatekeeping, 17–18, 20–2, 73
    mediation, 4, 5, 69
    politics, 23, 112, 129
    professionalism, xiii–xv, 8, 9,
        22–4, 27–41, 43–52,
        107–14, 128
    public, 7, 12, 23
    purchasing, 23, 43–4, 48–51
    qualifications, 108–10
    reference, xiii
    trust, 22
Library Association – see
    Chartered Institute of
    Library and Information
    Professionals
Library Association of New
    Zealand Aotearoa, 40
libertarianism, 20
libraries:
    academic, 43, 87
    buildings, 88
    case studies, 52–63, 74–84,
        96–106
    catalogues, 46–8
    location, 89
    membership, 90
    opening hours, 89
    public, 19, 23, 27, 43, 48–9,
        87, 94

school, 47
subject collections, 43
users, 12
library management systems, 49
library schools, 72, 108–9
library students, xx, 24
licences, 71
LMS – see library management
    systems
local government, 12
Local Government Act 1988, 12
Loch Ness Monster, 50–1

Magna Carta, 3
Mapplethorpe, Robert, 14, 19
moral indignation, xiv
My Child Is Psychic (TV
    programme), 51

National Library of Scotland, 95
National Security Letters, 9, 94–5
New Jersey, 94
New Zealand, 40
newspapers, 19, 27, 49
NSL – see National Security
    Letters

Of Mice and Men (novel), 49
outsourcing, 45

P2P – see file sharing
Patriot Act 2001, 9–10, 94–5
peer-to-peer technologies – see file
    sharing
personal information, 3, 5
Philippines, 38–9
phone calls, 3
photocopiers, 68, 73
photography, 14
plagiarism, 72–3
police, 14, 15

political parties, 12
pornography, 3, 14, 18, 20, 91
Portsmouth, 22
privacy, 10, 17–21, 30, 34, 35,
    89–95, 128
professional:
    development, xv, 24
    ethics, 11–25, 27–41, 43–52,
        107–14, 129
    literature, 109
    misconduct, 32, 34
    networks, xiv, 110–11
    revalidation, 109
professional associations, xiv
    ethical codes, 11, 13, 28–41
Professional Regulation
    Commission of the Republic
    of the Philippines:
    ethical code, 38–9
public domain, xiv
public:
    librarians, 7, 12, 23
    libraries, 19, 23, 27, 43, 48–9,
        87, 94
    publishers, 44

qualifications, 108–10

Ranganathan, S.R., 15, 86
    five laws, 15–16
reader development, 44
reference librarians, xiii
Regulation of Investigatory
    Powers Act 2000, 9
religion, 30, 36, 37, 47, 49–50
revalidation, 109
Rushdie, Salman, 49

Satanic Verses, The (novel), 49
satellites, 2, 3

school libraries, 47
Scottish Parliament, 27
September 11th, 10, 30, 90–1, 93,
    94–5, 129
sexual health, 18, 91
Shorley, Deborah, 10
Socrates, 1
software, 2
    licences, 71
spam, 90
Stonehenge, 3
Sturges, Paul, 14, 22, 27
subject collections, 43

terrorism, xiii, 10, 94–5
Terrorism Act 2006, 10, 95,
    129

UK – see United Kingdom
USA – see United States of
    America
United Kingdom, 32–4, 45, 66,
    67–8, 69, 88, 93, 95, 109
United States of America, 9,
    29–31, 47, 49, 72, 88, 94,
    129
universities, 67–8
University of New South Wales,
    68
University of North Texas School
    of Library and Information
    Science, 72

web pages, 2, 4
webcams, 2
western values, 16
Wikipedia, 50
Windows Media Player, 70

young people, 48–9

Printed in the United States
103318LV00002B/66/A